Interpretation First

Interpretation First

The Study Of All Beginnings

Paul Tarsleh

God has dealt with the earth in dispensations like He did in the Heavens.

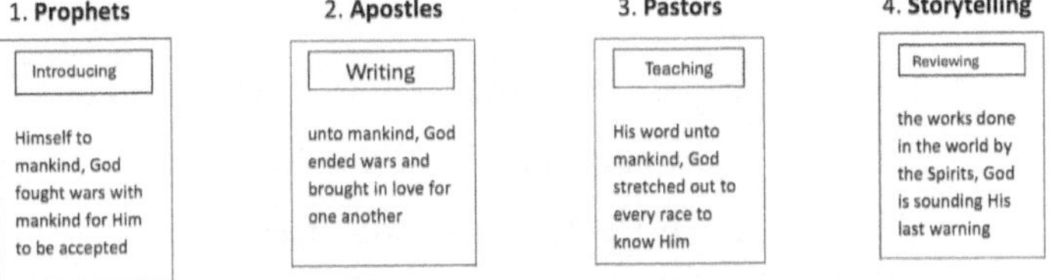

- **Time for teaching how to be righteous is over; it's quizzing and review time.** Remember that before a final exam in school, a teacher gives a quiz and a review. So, this is God's own time to quiz on what has been taught and review all that has been written. And before court action takes place, sometimes a judge gives legal advice, so this is God's own time to give His final advice.

- In this review, there are two Spiritual Truths that remain the secret things of the new world to come. God chooses to be silent on them due to some peculiar reasons.

- In this review, there is only one place previously chosen by God to be the peace center for all peoples to run to, to learn peace, but the people there have neglected peace talks and have lost their purpose in the world. God wants to defend Himself against some misunderstandings of His actions to them right now before the world. Therefore, let the world open its ears.

- Every Christian has heard about the narrow gate and how many are called, but few shall be chosen. Now is the time to define that narrow gate and how few shall be qualified among the many who're doing the work of God today.

- Every man knows how sweet the fish is, but not all know whether human poop makes the fish sweeter. This you'll know only when you open the fish's gut after it has just eaten poop. This is how the sweet things we do are made of poop [dirty things], but we don't see how dirty until now when God opens up the guts of our lives.

- Before the first world was destroyed, Noah was sent to advance God's warning. Now, I am that physical man to offer God's warning to physical men.

- Oh! See how pitiful it is to be rich and later turn poor; it's just how the world majority goes about enjoying the world in all of its riches [everything that glitters to the majority here in this world and they do every day], but the same way a majority of people shall suffer perpetual gnashing and grunting in heavenly prison while a very tiny number [like the few suffering on earth to do things right] shall rest in heavenly paradise.

These issues in this mission statement are brought to the people of the world in four major books, and this is just one of them.

Contents

Preface

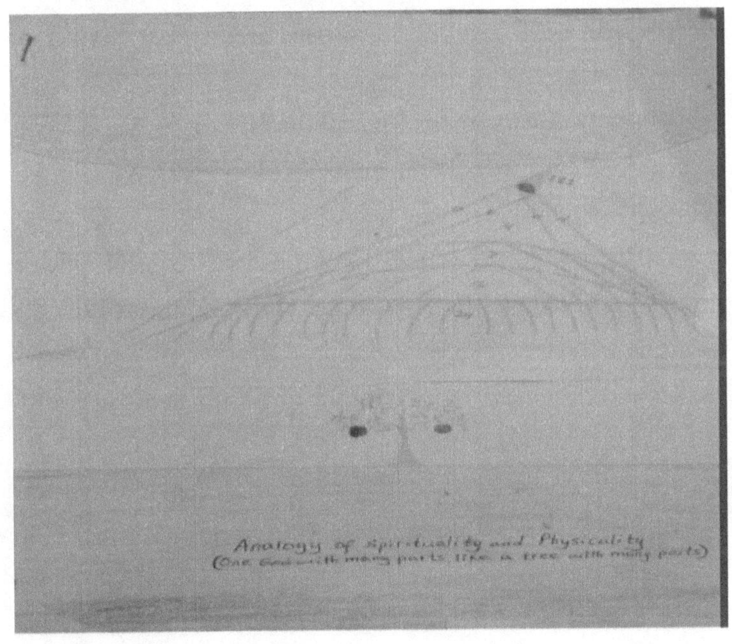

This book would simplify God and His spirits for us, which is why the diagram above depicts His evolvement, growth, and duplicity.

Since everything about Him is invisible to human eyes, the picture of a tree on earth would best explain Him to us.

Therefore, this manually prepared depiction is an analogy of Spirituality and Physicality [One invisible God protruding out of Heaven with many invisible parts {spirits/forces (angels)} like a visible tree with many parts (trunk, branches, stems, leaves, and fruits)] standing on the ground.

We (humans) cannot see God and His angels or angles [God's Angel- means His "Angle/Extension"], but there is a lot that we will learn about them in this last period of revision.

There are many questions and doubts about who God is or whether He truly exists or if He does, then who made Him or where did He come from.

To discuss all these questions, we need to begin with a little drill: Let's ask ourselves some questions about how the ground (soil) on which we walk came about, and then we ask ourselves again how the trees that grow on it came about; who made them all?

Finding answers to these questions could help us answer the questions about how Heaven came about and how God evolved out of that Heaven.

Although there are no answers to how Heaven or He came about, we can use our imagination to understand the evolution of the trees and grasses.

Isn't it a mystery when we wake up in the morning and

see grasses and plants growing on the very spot that we used a Bulldozer to clear yesterday?

I believe science students would quickly jump at it to say the plants grew out of the seeds and the roots that have been lying in the soil a long time or that some seeds were blown onto the ground by wind or dropped by some birds and insects flying over but to say any one of these would open another question on the science students. They will have to answer a question like; who made those seeds and roots that have been lying under the soil there or dropped by those flying creatures? Another question would be, who made those creatures flying over the place? Eventually, there would be an unending question-and-answer process, which is why it is foolish to make any attempt to find His evolvement.

SO, HOW IT ALL HAPPENED?

Unfortunately, no one knows who made the first Heaven to which God is connected in the picture above. It is the only thing among creations that has no source of creator. Thus, we can only say it just came about.

To heavenly dwellers, it stares in their faces every day like we see the soil staring in our faces everywhere we go in our world, too.

Therefore, after so many years had passed, a shoot sprang out of that Heaven, and it became known as God. This word stands for *"**Go Out** to **D**emonstrate."*

Therefore, His evolution is like a plant shoot that shows up on an empty ground one morning after a few days when a bulldozer had cleared the ground. Like the plant shoot [say orange plant shoot] that elongates by hours, so did the Spirit of God in Heaven elongate by years.

But a tree grows upward, looking for the sunlight, while the Spirit of the Lord God grows downward, looking for the earth He created afterwards.

Often, after several days, a plant shoot curdles [Ossify] to form a hard part called a joint where the tree prepares to divide into branches, which is the same as God did when He formed the red-looking ball, as the picture above shows. Later, the ball-like area would be called "Jesuit," meaning junction or joint, now known as Jesus. It was God's resting point before He created His angles, now angels.

The Angels live in other places to work

Now, God had made the angels like an agriculturist who made a nursery, and God had to create other areas for them to live in so they could do many jobs.

Also, like an agriculturist who transports soil from one point to another to create special soil types, so did God in his ability to create several other places (layers or spheres) outside the first Heaven. He created the first layer He called "heaven or firmament." That's why the Book of Genesis says: "God made the firmament and divided the *waters* which were under the firmament from the waters which were above the firmament; and it was so. "And God called the firmament *Heaven*" (Gen. 1:7 NKJV).

The many spirits of God

Still, using the analogy of a tree, we can easily understand the many parts of God called His spirits.

At the joint of a tree comes some protrusions, and they become branches to which other little branches connect and to them some stems and to the stems are leaves and fruits, and even the leaves have veins. This is how God divided Himself into many large, medium, small, and tiny spirits He would refer to as Archangels, Angels, and the spirits (the ones moving around daily, hourly, by minutes, and by seconds, even split seconds).

We, humans, fall under God's creation category of solid parts after He had grown longer until He became hard, harder, and hardest. The hardest are the metals.

The Spirits are good and bad (obedient and disobedient)

At some point, the fruits of a tree grow ripe, and some rot or some parts rot, while other fruits are good for eating.

So, when the owner goes to pick fruits from his tree, he often discards some [the spoiled ones] and takes some [the good ones] for food.

The angels and humans are the fruits of God while He is the trunk or vine, and they all have rotten ones and good ones that God, the owner, shall separate when He comes to harvest. The fruit analogy describing angels and humans to God is how they become beneficial to Him.

As for the Spirit of God that hangs over the earth, It [He] broke up into four (4) large other Spirits/Angles (a,b,c,d), and by human science, they're known as the Heat (Sun), the Cold (Moon), the Rain (Water) and the Darkness [Spiritually they're the Four Spirits/Angels around God's Throne in Heaven].

The first three are well understood, but Darkness reaches the earth as death and sleep. [Death to God is not an evil spirit but a spirit of undoing {deconstructing} what is done {constructed}].

The Spirit of Death operates [owns] several departments. That's why it comes in many forms, such as infections and retrieval of life.

A keen look at the diagram above tells you there are seven (7) other spirits reporting to the four while twelve (12) other spirits report to the seven spirits, and finally, twenty-four (24) other spirits that control so many little spirits are found reporting to the twelve superior ones.

These are the branches of the one big God. Among them are the evil ones (Satan and his collaborators).

The earth's inhabitants do not see the spirits, but they can feel them as a breeze that blows their bodies or as air that goes in and out of their bodies. Inhabitants of the earth may also hear them like the thundering wind and the lightning. They're both peaceful and destructive in all their works.

Introduction

The Trinity

That one [#1]God [tiny in the eyes of man from the earth) has a second [#2]part and other [#3]spirits, and it reads as God (the father/first), the Son (Second), and the Holy Spirit [Perfect Spirit but should be other spirits.]

So, the red ball to which the four connect is called Jesuit (First of the angles or branches), now called "Jesus." The other angels also called him "Khist" to be "God's Shadow," which later became known as "Christ."

As clearly seen in the diagram, no one or no message goes to the first (father) except through the second (Son) of Him. It is the same as saying nothing goes to the trunk/roots of a tree except through the Joint (Junction) to which the primary branches are connected, and the same goes for saying that nothing goes to the branches except through the junction.

Therefore, the father (First) and the Son (Second) are the same [the one {1} become two {2}.]

God's hierarchical order

The diagram is the hierarchy of heavenly government.

Some of these spirits of God herein distinguished as the evil ones are doing so many marvelous things in the world of humankind, and as such, their deeds must be fully revealed.

This book, therefore, looks at them in three major categories; the men's world, the women's world, and the government systems they taught on earth with their subsidiaries, all captioned in chapters.

The best I can say to this effect is that this book is the genesis of all my books and is a retelling of the very things that happened long ago in the Spirit Realm between God and Lucifer/Satan. This time, they're rewritten using the prose style but not the poetry.

This book is a detailed account of spiritual matters, more than what is said in the Bible.

So, I wouldn't be surprised at all if theologians view it as speculative or imaginative since they've been used to teaching only what they have been taught over the centuries.

This book is the best way to understand the Bible and the powers dictating our activities today.

Other things about this book

One other important point I need to make before jumping into chapter one is that this book contains social issues ranging from the way Christians live their lives together with non-Christians all the way to government systems such as Communism and Democracy that may be very homogeneous to what you see and hear around the world today, so much real that you may think that I, the writer of these things, have deviated from Spirituality and went into politics of the earth. But no, I'm not discussing earthly matters. Rather, the Spirit of God does.

It/He [the Spirit/the Man] says politics or governing systems you see today have been the expression or repurposing of what God does in Heaven, but He [God] blends them together to work perfectly to make Heaven look good and free of sins. Heaven here refers to where God resides.

So, the purpose of reporting them as exactly as they are today is to point out how useless it is for nations to condemn one another's ideas rather than appreciating them and using them to strengthen each system of things wherever you find them.

This is especially true when the world is nearing a well-advanced robotic stage, when certain jobs performed by thousands of humans shall [should] be done by these robots, thereby causing job scarcity.

However, under robotic science, would Communist/Socialist ideas find it easier to take care of its citizens.

This is the kind of discussion God wants to initiate

among mankind. So, God gave unto me, the writer but not author, these things to write.

And before I close, I want to point out that there is other information in this book that was taken from other sources, such as the scientific definition of 'yawn' and for this, some people may expect a bibliography, but since we now live in the internet age, let Google be my reference.

Finally, sometimes, as a reader, you may encounter a phrase like 'the man who told me this': when this happens, I want you to know that I'm simply referring to Christ or any one of His spirits [messengers who came down to me on His behalf] since almost all the characters of my books are spirits. So, wherever there is human character, I shall indicate that.

Sometimes, you shall find two different spellings for the same word 'Spirit' as 'spirit,' in which case the capital 'S' will always be referencing the Spirit of God Himself while the lower 's' will always reference a messenger of God or Christ.

Therefore, in this book and all my books, please stop wasting your time on checking the conventional way to spell some words you're familiar with because I'm writing directly under the instruction of the Man who gave me His work to do.

Chapter One

The gods of our lands

The topic, "The gods of our lands," refers to the lower powers of the Great God. They're the gods or supernatural powers that established the systems every tribe or nation referred to as cultures and traditions they have. These were/are the gods people worshipped/worship as oracles or shrines or temples to tell fortunes, administer healings, or commit evils.

In my tribe, they have long known two gods, even before Christianity (Monotheism) reached them. Even though they really worshipped many gods, but they called them the pepper-eating gods [gods that are fed with pepper food] while they recognized one big God whom they say lives in Heaven.

For those who administer herbs, they will say everything will be fine if the heavenly God agrees.

So, I had little knowledge of this Heavenly God before I began to go to church, first with my grandmother and then later with my grandfather while I was yet a little boy in my hometown.

In church, the focus of whom to devote your worship is the big God.

This big God everybody talks about is neither seeable nor touchable. He is a Spirit. A Spirit is an invisible (Not seeable by the naked eyes of human beings) character of a person or thing.

The characteristics of a spirit are beyond the imagination of human beings.

The Spirit or spirits can change shape (size and length) and color. The spirits can fly, contract, or cut, then repair themselves.

These different abilities of a spirit were given to me to make it simple to understand by observing all the things done in human science because the Spirit of God is science in physical manifestation.

When the spirit [spirit of any lower god] begins to affect the human body or human life in either a harmful way or helpful way, it takes up different names like disease and mineral and like weapons or equipment.

The big God has children but no wife. He made them just like science today does to make Teddies.

As human science [human's ability to make things too] has grown to its peak, it has begun to make robots, which makes mankind assume the ability to create things in their likeness that would help do 99% of what he [mankind] does with his/her hands, just as God did when He made the angels and humans to do all His works.

The robots will communicate and move around just as we do every day. And when that happens, then will mankind understand who/what God is and what His angels are to Him. It is by then that Christians shall have the full understanding of who Lucifer (Now Satan) was to God, for which He (God) didn't take away His (God's) power from him (Satan).

For I have been made to understand that God is the creator of the angels (the lower spirits, both male and female), and they are His tools, equipment, and instruments. He uses them for His own purpose of doing whatever He wants to do.

Although He uses them, He gives them the ability to think and decide for themselves. And by this ability of self-decision-making [self-will power], Satan chose his own path, and other angels followed him [let's take Satan's case to be a situation in which a robot begins to malfunction and starts to destroy things all by itself while its owner tries to find a way to arrest the situation.]

By the time Lucifer deflected from the Wills of God, the Wills of his father and creator, there were both men and women spirits in Heaven, but only the men spirits fought a war with him in Heaven, so they alone ran away from the dwelling (Holy) place of God. These are the spirits (all men) that came down to Earth.

The word "Earth" that is referred to in this case was not the literal one we human beings walk on today, but it refers to a mass of air that is hanging right above the physical ground [that's why it is spelled with capital 'E' wherever it appears in a sentence while the physical earth is lower 'e'].

The voice that gave me this story gave me the word "Lithosphere" to refer to a mass of air that hosts the forces that control our physical ground and all that it contains. [In human science, this Lithosphere is defined as "the solid outer layer of the earth above the asthenosphere, consisting of the crust and upper mantle," but the Spirit had already told me that everything on earth has a Spiritual representative or root in the Spirit Realm because physical things are all replica of Spiritual things and that means every single word on earth is there in the Spirit Realm and that includes the word "Lithosphere."]

For example, there is water in Heaven:

"And he showed me a pure river of water of life, clear as crystal, proceeding out of the throne of God and of the Lamb." "Verse2 In the midst of the street of it, and on either side of the river, was there the tree of life, which bare twelve manners of fruits, and yielded her fruit every month: and the leaves of the tree were for the healing of the nations."

— (Rev.22:1-2 KJV.)

This is a sample of Spiritual waters that serve as the fountain of waters on earth.

There are also minerals in Heaven as on earth:

"You were in Eden, the garden of God; every precious stone adorned you: carnelian, chrysolite and emerald, topaz, onyx and jasper, lapis lazuli, turquoise and beryl. Your settings and mountings were made of gold; on the day you were created, they were prepared."

— (Ezk. 28:13).

There are trees in Heaven as on earth. (Read Rev. 22:2 again as above.) Even there are streets as in the same Rev. 22:2.

So, such names given to anything on earth once came from the Spirit that put that word on the tongue of a man or a woman living on earth.

So, you see, Satan is a Spirit, and we don't see him even while he is with us. His invisibility is proof that the world in which he lives away from God, his father, is also an invisible world. That's why when the Christian book of the Bible says Satan came down to earth, it is not talking about physicality, but the mass of air that blows our bodies in the form of breeze is that Earth in which he resides.

This close location to human beings that Satan has has afforded him a greater opportunity to interact with physical beings more than other spirits of God do.

So, he (Satan) and his group of men that came to Earth formed their own Kingdom with a system of doing things that they called "Government/governing system."

He became the Head of that government, and He assigned various tasks to others who also became local leaders of others. Together, they made their own laws and regulations as to how to rule the world and they became the Custodians of the Laws that govern their activities to be carried on in the world.

I want to tell you the different activities of these gods, how they created the system of things human beings use, and they call them "cultures and traditions" all around the world that define one particular group of people from another, but I first want to explain why God actually created these forces/spirits and created humans too because these are the two similar but different creations of His that are doing so many new things even beyond His own expectations now.

Chapter Two

God's purpose for creating angels and human beings

There are two major Estates God had created, the Heavens and the earth, each with its own subdivisions. The Heavens is a Spiritual kind which means everything in it is soft or gaseous. There, He needs tools and equipment to enhance His work, and He needs instruments to amuse Himself at times. So, God made them, and He called them "Angels", literally means "Angles/extensions/helpers." They're also soft and gaseous like He is.

Other than God's gaseous state, He needs a stronger part to support Him and that brings in the creation of the earth. The earth (The sum of all natural things that the earth's crust contains) also needs stronger (Muscular) forces to cultivate/maintain it, and that brings in the creation of human beings.

So, the purpose of the angels is to enhance the work of God in Heaven, while the purpose of human beings is to enhance the work of the Spirit (God and His angels) on earth. This means angels are tools to God as human beings are tools to the Spirit.

Now, an angel is the replica of God as a human being is their (The angels and God's) replica. Just as God taught the angels some skills to work in Heaven, so have the angels taught human beings some skills to work on earth.

Now, human beings have reached the stage of creating robots after their own kind to enhance their work on earth. The cycle of creation has come to an end, thus producing a formula of creational ability like this:

God (A powerful Force) on
Angel (A powerful Force) on
Human (A powerful Force) on
Robot.

So, these angels (The rebel forces) of God took Man to themselves after God had thrown them (Both Man and Satan) out of Heaven or out of His sight, and Man began to live with them (Satan and his men) who trained him (Man) into artworks.

Before we go any further, let me make clear that the kind of man I'm talking about right now is not a physical man yet [that's why the word "Man" is spelled with a capital 'M' to denote His Spirituality]. He is that Spiritual Man my second book about Noah's Ark refers to as the Soul of man [that immortal/cannot die part of the human body]: "And when he had opened the fifth seal, I saw under the alter the Souls of them that were slain for the word of God" (Rev. 6:9 KJV). "Do not be afraid of those who kill the body but cannot kill the Soul. Rather, be afraid of the one who can destroy both the Soul and body in hell" (Matt. 10:28 NIV).

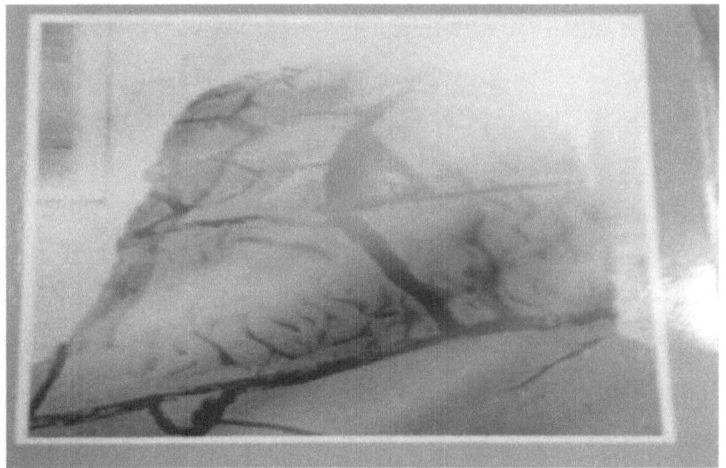

This is the kind of Man that will later germinate in the soil during the rain (Flood Time) and evolve (come out) of the mud after the rain (After the Flood had subsided) to become a living being.

Man evolving out of the ground

Spiritual existences

Let's hear what the church of Latter Day's Saints says about this man.

In their book, they have a topic, "*Where did I come*

from?" written on page 2 of a Bible teaching Tract that has the title "The Plan of Salvation." In there, they write, "Your life didn't begin at birth, nor will it end at death. You are made up of a spirit body (sometimes called the soul) and a physical body. Your Heavenly Father created your spirit, and you lived with Him as a spirit before you were born on earth. You knew and loved Him, and He knew and loved you. This period is called *pre-earth life.*"

The Christian book also referenced this kind of man in Gen. 2:7: "Then the Lord God formed man from the dust of the ground and breathed into his nostrils the breath of life, and the man became a living being."

Some spirits whispered to some scientists, such as British Marine Biologist Sir Alister Hardy, who attempted the aquatic theory. Since it has something to do with Spirituality, he couldn't prove it physically, which is why it didn't get widespread attention. However, after listening to the Spirit of God in 2008 concerning how mankind evolved, I concluded that his aquatic theory was connected to the Noah Flood parable in the Bible. My other book, *The Book of Interpretation Second*, has more on the first man and his evolution.

This is why the image above represents the evolution of the Spiritual man out of the mud into physicality, with the mud consisting of his flesh and all that is physical to see and touch.

Therefore, God told me in 2008 that all the things that I was taught [in the school of the Spirit of God] from 2006 to mid-2008 have been written about by the people who came before me, but their works contained some lapses (gaps) that

He [God] has come to correct and fill now during this review period.

Therefore, on the things of man's Spiritual existence, God brought forth to me Ezekiel 28:13-17 to begin the history of Satan's existence in the Garden of Eden where he did wrong things [assumed God's authority and deceived man] before he was thrown down to the earth.

So, the spirits of God started giving me the details on this Spiritual man by starting [first] with Lucifer [now Satan] in the Garden of Eden and his interaction there with man.

They [the many spirits that came down on earth to me one after another as lecturers on various issues] said to me that everything about today's mission, which is to review the Bible [go all over the Bible], hangs entirely on our complete understanding of the Garden of Eden which is the place of many activities at the beginning of all beginnings.

So, you see why my new books are here to make clear to everyone that everything and every name on earth has its root in the Spirit Realm, and whatever exists on earth is a replica. Or let me say it this way: before the physical earth was formed, there was a picture of this earth (its architectural design) that existed in Heaven in which God had already mapped out everything according to how He would want it to be. That Map of a Spiritual Earth in which God showed the greenness and all that was scheduled in it is what the Christian book called the Garden of Eden. That is why God made us understand in Ezekiel 28:13-17 that Satan was in there (In Eden, the garden of God) perfect and blameless until pride entered him, and he rebelled and, in verse 17, God said He threw him (Satan) down, to the ground.

Now, let's continue.

So, Satan and his group of men, having established their own Kingdom in the Spirit Realm, which borders with the earth's crust, began to train Man (the Spiritual Man) in arts and crafts, the skill/knowledge of making things which we now refer to on earth as human science.

This further explains that the seeds of arts and crafts were planted in that Spiritual Man while He was yet with Satan so that we're born with that knowledge of doing things, which is evidenced in the behavior of children when they try to make things earlier before they're completely taught or given better instructions as to how to make things look better.

It is the difference in how much knowledge each person obtains in the Spiritual World that makes some people more crafty or creative than others. All they need is the best opportunity and tools to fully express that sufficient gift embedded in them.

Because the seed of creativity is embedded in all peoples, including black people, some blacks became inventors in the Western world after receiving exposure to the right environment, education, tools, or equipment. Likewise, many races from around the world to the Western world, where high knowledge is cultivated, thus creating the right environment for nurturing and growth, get to grow the seeds of scientific knowledge quickly.

Do you remember the Bible story that says that Satan gave the fruit of Knowledge of good and evil to man in the Garden of Eden? Oh yes, he did. But what did that fruit really symbolize? Now I tell you, it symbolized the knowledge of how to make things.

Do you also remember that after they (Adam and Eve) had eaten the fruit of Knowledge of good and evil, they both obtained the sense of manufacturing or making things all by themselves? Oh yes, they gained the knowledge of making clothes after their eyes had opened and they saw themselves naked/nude, so they sewed fig leaves and covered themselves.

So, when God saw them in clothes, He wept and pitied them and reluctantly fulfilled them with the full knowledge of making things by giving them good clothes, which He called "garments."

Then God sent both (Satan and man) out of His presence to go and live and do things on their own.

But the Spirit of God said to me: God's decision to send man out with Lucifer was His angry way of entrusting man to Satan so that Satan would take charge of Man and let man suffer to learn a lesson of being disobedient.

So, while Man was under adoption, Satan and his group also inspired Man with the knowledge of how to rule; today, we call it a government system.

All the skills, attitudes, and behaviors that each of us exhibits right after birth are the total sum of the kind of knowledge that we obtained before birth. These inborn skills, attitudes (approaches like defiance or arrogance), and behaviors (conduct or manners) define the level of induction (how much training) each person received in the Kingdom of Satan before he/she was born.

To a lesser extent, we learn them from others. In some instances, they could be suppressed by our type of parents or guardians and friends and the kind of society we may be exposed to after birth.

Depending on the level of suppression or relief we receive, we tend to hide or grow our attitudes and behaviors. Let me make it simple: a wayward child with very harsh parents who give severe punishments all the time for the slightest offense committed will tend to be a good child whenever the parents are around, but away, oops, everything comes right outside.

We will discuss this more when we discuss cultures and traditions. I will then take you through a list of activities Satan and his group, known as "The gods of our lands," have been responsible for throughout the ages.

As glittering as they may seem today, Jesus condemned all of these during his short stay on earth. He said all of them would pass away, and a new world would come.

But before getting there, let me talk a little bit about the structure of these gods.

You already know that Satan is their head, so the Spirit of God commanded me to make clear that whatever the Christian book calls "Powers and Principalities in High Places" describes four great demons Satan appointed to the four major corners of the earth. [Demon is the short form of *Demonstrator*].

But before them, Satan has one archangel [his immediate agent] called "Alasaman," who oversees the four great demons called the Councilmen—the four Councilmen report to Satan through Alasaman.

The four often receive reports from seven other demons overseeing the seven great land masses (Continents) of the earth. The seven may be rightfully referred to as Satan's Ministers of Lands.

These land ministers are responsible for appointing local leaders for every country in the world. I suppose you can now imagine how the chain of government is drawn down to who is accountable for each clan in our District. All these terminologies came about each time there was a need to extend responsibilities for any apparent reason.

Chapter Three

The homage system of the gods

Way back in the beginning, in Heaven, Satan, then Lucifer, was one of God's original angels. He was one of God's original tools or equipment before many other angels were created. These tools or equipment would later be called God's robots at the advanced level when they were made capable of speaking and thinking in Heaven.

As a tool [robot] for God to use to do His work, He (God) had to train [sharpen] him like the two other original ones. So, Satan, Lucifer then, acquired a great wealth of knowledge or skills from his father, God.

So, as the only original angel who broke away or split from his father, he was the most knowledgeable of all the angels that came down. This qualified him, even up to date, as the only one among the rebels now ruling us, to have as much power as God does.

The homage system

So, to remain feared and respected by all, he instituted a system he called something-for-something or give-and-take.

Under this system, each of the four subordinates must pay respect [homage] to him. A Homage- is an honorable visit to the Headquarters where Satan lives. During such visit, the visitor, being the lower order/servant, must bring a lot of goodies to the boss.

Upon the presentation of any gift(s), the boss makes an assessment to determine how good or satisfying the gifts are. Upon his assessment and appraisal, he grants the visitor a chance to make a request for whatever the visitor wants. And in his (the boss's) determination and willingness, he grants the visitor a gift, which comes in the form of additional power to the visitor or requester.

So, upon returning, the four Councilmen, who often visit Headquarters once every year, do the same to their seven subordinates and the seven to their country representatives, and the chain continues to the least clan leaders.

The question now is, what kind of gift do they carry to the boss? Now, I come to reveal the importance of the earth's materials and their uses to the Spirit.

God's purpose for creating the earth's materials

The resources of the earth [the plants, mammals, fishes, and birds] are made for food, not only for human beings as it appeared earlier to mankind but also for the Spirit, except in two different ways.

It is a cycle in which human beings eat the above-mentioned things, digest them [break them into soluble {here means, 'soften parts'}], and then the spirit enters the human body to feed on, taking nourishment to those who keep the system in Heavens running.

So, the forces of God assigned on earth transport food and other things from earth to the Heavens.

Because we're made not to see them, so we don't see them, but we feel them entering and leaving our bodies as the air we inhale and exhale.

The purpose of the Spirit feeding on mankind is the reason God spoke of the human body as His temple, which is why He would say mankind must keep the body holy. *The Book of Interpretation Fourth* reveals more about this in sex issues.

Why did God warn about the misuse of the body?

Just like both good people and bad people go to every public place in our towns and cities in this world, so are the demons (bad spirits) and angels (good spirits) who enter God's public building (the human body) to do whatever they want from there. And just like a city containing several factory machines to make food and other things for us, so is the human body [God's factory] containing several machines to make food and other things for the spirits.

This means that from the plants, mammals, fish, and birds we eat come "minerals," which contain energy and power that Heaven needs to run.

Since humans are complex machines (giant robots) that God has on earth to process things before they are taken to Heaven, humans must receive the same energy to function well and get things ready for shipment. That's why all the spirits have access to this earthly machine of God.

What does human sacrifice mean?

Hahaha! There was an outburst of laughter before the spirit answered this question, and I can't refuse to do the same.

Remember your Bible story that says the human body is made of the dust of the ground? The human body, therefore, contains a high content of these minerals, which is why the spirit desires the human body, herein referred to as the flesh and bones that can dissolve back into the ground when life has been taken out.

The different storage areas of energy

The energy they take from us can be found in our blood, flesh, bone, brain, and sexual fluids. These are the various storage areas of the energy we derive from our daily eating.

Therefore, the demon spirits largely derive their food [that means the energy stored in the food] from our flesh and blood, which is why human sacrifices are required in every part of the world in different forms.

That's why, in ancient times, and even in some parts of the world today, the talk about offering human blood or parts to shrines or oracles explains this theory.

In Western countries and growing-technology countries, wars in all their forms do explain the same demand for human flesh and blood for the demon world.

I mean, the practice of offering more gifts [essentially human blood] to the Spirit world often receives reciprocation that is still going on even in the so-called "civilized" world where human killing is so common with the people and knowledge is dispensed among them more than any other peoples used to receive around the world. [This should now explain why the Western world exists above others today. This means that due to their continuous desire for wars through technology, they have been spilling blood and unknowingly making sacrifices to the gods, which has always been reciprocated by more scientific knowledge coming to them. But recently, the Spirit world has started expanding science to others due to other factors, like more inquisitions from the hearts of other people affected by these acts of wars, etc.].

[Satan really uses human blood or flesh to avoid the complications involved in the primary method. The complication is a fight that ensues whenever His agents enter to dip from the sexual bowl of the human body. The sexual bowl means that human sexual fluids contain the energy that the Spirit world needs.] *The Interpretation Fourth* book has more on this.

But the angels, on the other hand, do focus on the primary method [the sexual fluids of man and woman] to receive the energy contained in all the minerals of the earth, which is taken from the human body after the body has received the energy through the food we eat to make mineral deposits into the human semen [the male's sperm and the female's egg]. This condition has been the major secret behind God's demand for virginity before marriage and faithfulness after marriage.

But God is starving today when a random lifestyle has become the order of the day. His angels hardly find the preserved and the faithful, even among Christians.

Initially, the angels used to feed from the matured virgins; both unmarried males and females who had not had sex yet were called the clean ones. But as the married men who became polygamists began to pollute women when they slept with one woman to another while demanding faithfulness from the women, Christian women and men who heeded the word of God to remain virgins before marriage and remain faithful after marriage became the source of energy for the angels. But as promiscuity has become prevalent among all in the last days, the angels hardly find anyone to extract their food to carry to Heaven, which is why God is starving.

The quest for these thicker minerals [thicker like the brain part of an animal] is the reason for wars in the world by which these demons kill human beings all the time. Some have become wasteful, so much so that they kill unnecessarily. These wasteful ones need fresh food all the time, just like those people today who think they have so much money, so they don't need to eat leftover food but waste it always to get fresh food.

These wasteful demons are the ones causing physical

fights in our homes and in all its forms that result in deaths around the world.

Before getting to discuss scientific accomplishments on earth, I must inject here that the vast and fast need for human nutrients has continued to push mankind into the invention of more weapons of mass destruction.

Chapter Four

Why did the Spirit require virginity and faithful marriage?

Wars to kill human beings had been the original tactic of the male spirits (Satan's demons), while the good spirits of God (the angels) concentrated on obtaining their energy from the semen of every human being.

This reservoir of rich nutrients in the human body was considered the cleanest source of energy food for the Kingdom of God [The spheres of Heavens in which the angels and God Himself dwell]. For this secret (sacred) reason, God Himself instituted the virginity and faithful marriage code of law.

Under this code of law, a mature man (both male and female) was required to stay out of sex until marriage. After marriage, they two were required to remain committed/faithful to each other. Still, Satan, being the spirit of division and partiality, chose only women to stay virgins before marriage [let's wait until we start a discussion on the topic "Marriage"].

Instead, Satan made the male humans marry as many wives as they could since the women were deemed the property of the men. This is Satan's teaching of the scripture that says the woman was created out of the man's rib bone, which he calls the woman being the man's property that man can use any way he likes.

Also, the woman must be subjected to obedience; she must remain faithful, respectful, dutiful, and a servant. These were all enshrined in marriage laws in ancient days before God came down to earth to take Abraham from the village of Ur.

That is why God did not institute marriage in the human world. Rather, God foresaw what Satan was planning to do to the woman [take her from her parents and give her unto a man as a property for the man] and predicted it, unlike the way the Bible writers understood it from Moses' writings.

So, under the homage system, the lower powers carry these various nutrients as gifts from earth to Heaven (to Satan's own Enclave or sphere of the Milky World). They obtain them from human beings through the method I've already mentioned.

War among them the gods

The homage system Satan instituted among his servants created a competition among the gods. It was and is a competition to obtain more power.

It is the root of internal wrangling among the gods. This means that every leader endeavors harder to gain favor from his boss, to get more power, and to do more things on earth all the time. In the process, the unintended result is a fierce fight amongst the gods/spirits/forces operating on the earth, affecting the physical human body or a territorial arena where each power exercises control.

Their rule on earth (Satan's Divide and Rule System)

1. Different Cultures and Traditions

These spirits are called the "gods of our lands" because they divided themselves to oversee the activities of man all over the earth. They made man organize different forms of government in various world locations.

The lifestyle that each group of people had [still has] to live as their governing system was arranged under a set of rules and regulations called laws, and these laws became known as every group's own culture (Cutteur/cultivate) and tradition (trading/move around). This means these laws were cultivated/cut alongside God's Laws and are bound to be traded/moved around the world's peoples.

Therefore, the true meaning of "Culture and Tradition"

is "Laws and their Movements." This also means these laws are not very different from God's Laws in Heaven except that they have been corrupted (changed in some ways to reflect the selfish desires of these rebel forces.) For example, God freely gives everything to all. No one owns anything in Heaven except God, the creator and owner of all. That's why no buying and selling exist in Heaven [the sphere God resides in], but rather, everyone goes to the cafeteria [they called it "Cafeteet"] to serve himself/herself any food he/she wants.

Food Centers in Heaven are exactly like Buffets on earth, where everyone serves himself/herself whatever he/she likes by picking from the varieties of food prepared by cooks.

You see why I like the things I heard from the Spirit. In my home country, Liberia, I had never visited a buffet, and I didn't even know if it existed in my country until 2014 when I left there to come to America. So, I didn't know what it looked like in a Buffet. Still, I learned from the Spirit that such restaurants exist on earth where people serve themselves as much food as they want, except that people pay money in Buffets in our world before serving themselves. At the same time, no one has to pay money before getting any food in Heaven.

The reason is that money is used for something else in Heaven rather than a medium of exchange, but on earth, Satan and his agents have maintained the purpose but changed the uses of money [we shall get to that later]. And for anything other than food that anyone wants, that is what he/she gets freely from a general shopping Center now referred to as a "Mall" on earth. So, let's find out where the money comes from and what money is.

Chapter Five

Origin of money

Money in Heaven is used to honor high-ranking officials with titles. A photo of such an official, like all the archangels of God, is minted and printed for distribution among all for official recognition. It has no other use in Heaven except to honor and recognize or identify a high-ranking leader of God.

So, when Satan established his Enclave, his own Kingdom outside God's, and instituted the Give-and-Take system of doing things in the world, he chose to use the money for the same purpose of being seen and recognized by all, but this time, he used it as a medium of exchanging things in the world.

But before minting and printing coins and papers, he introduced the Give-Me-What-You-Have and I Give-You-

What-You-Lack system, which was called the "Barter System," which meant to say, "Let's exchange."

Under the Barter System, there were no specific things like "Money" for everyone to look for; it was purely based on any material like pepper or orange that a particular person lacked and wanted from another who, too, lacked and wanted a clay pot or a machete [a machete is called *cutlass* in Africa]. In that case, the two would have to discuss determining how much orange is needed for what quantity of clay pot to exchange.

This kind of exchange talk brought in a word called "Bargain," which means the "Border between our gains/wants."

The barter system started as an individual-based thing, then grew into a community-level matter when community leaders began to get involved in settling disputes arising from arguments of disagreement over the determination of how much person A wanted to give for what he wanted to get and how much person B wanted to accept for what he had. The word 'Community' means "Commune/come together."

Have you noticed I'm not using the pronoun "She" here? That is because, at that time, women were not allowed to make deals or transact businesses. They were mere wives who sat home to watch the men do everything that concerned everyone's survival.

Community leaders' involvement in settling exchange disputes entrusted them with the responsibility of determining the value (quantity) of exchange for everything that existed within their borders.

Please let me clarify that the word "Community" herein refers to the word "village/town." When a town began to exchange some things with another town, the bargaining (exchange talks) grew to an advanced level, and the word "Trade," which means "Move Around," came in.

Somehow, along the way, the idea of having something pressure to use for exchange came in, and different long-lasting materials were discovered to be used in this manner. That's how pressure stones came in, notably Gold, a shining stone that could be kept for a lifetime.

Now that gold was a stone that Blacksmiths could heat to refine/change its shape, the drawing of images on gold then came in and brought the word "Money" to earth wherein the Heads of leaders of various societies (groups of towns/villages) were printed for circulation to be seen by all people under their control.

Eventually, the advent of technology led to the printing of a leader's picture on a distinctly prepared paper known as Money. This idea was sparked by complaints of the heaviness people felt when moving gold coins from place to place.

This discussion of money in our world today is to tell you how Satan's ugly (cunning/tricky) behaviors always copy something that is true in God's Kingdom and how he can use that thing differently in his (Satan's) Kingdom. In this particular case, the printing and distribution of the Heads of leaders is very accurate with money in Heaven. Still, its use as a medium/means of obtaining food and everything else in our world is false.

In Heaven, money is not a prerequisite for receiving anything one needs from God. Remember your scriptures telling you how God freely gives us all things. Whether you are good or bad, we all receive the air to breathe, the rain for water, the sun for heating, and everything else. This is also true about what and how heavenly dwellers freely receive all things in Heaven.

By introducing an ownership system in our world through the search for one particular thing, which was his picture for all of his agents to see in his Enclave and the photos of all of his subordinates who rule over the earth for all their human subjects to see, the money system became the best trap for all to bow under his rule and thus remain his slaves who beg for monetary blessings every day.

And yet he got these different spirits (demonic agents) that are deployed all over the place to cause havoc in every man's direction, such as sicknesses and disasters that demand money to solve.

This is to say that using several manipulations by which every individual is held in bondage, such as the induction into an extreme desire for sex, drunkenness, and other obscene behaviors, have always caused men and women of this world to help Satan achieve a particular desire. We shall see what these desires are later in subsequent times.

Chapter Six

Governing system as ownership

As I mentioned earlier, everything in our human world is a copy of something God created at the beginning of beginnings. Still, when Lucifer broke away, he took along with him everything God taught him and the other angels. So, when he (Lucifer, now Satan) founded his kingdom, he began to use God's systems, but this time, he started to repurpose them to his advantage. This is why many things originating from Satan seem like they're from God or they're of God. One such thing is the governing system.

So, as we dive into this topic, don't forget that Satan and his men were the powers of the air who started the world order that became known as cultures and traditions around the world. This is the reason Jesus didn't favor the Jews' cultures and traditions they claimed were given to them by his father, God, the Almighty. They didn't know God only allowed them to continue with the cultures and traditions He met on earth.

So, the system of governing or ruling people falls under the cultural and traditional ways of human life.

In the old days, people were made Kings for a lifetime, and Kingship was given to a particular family/household. The practice of kingship was taken from Heaven, where God reigns as a King forever and ever.

Kingship started as an honor to someone who performed a heroic act during a war against another kingdom. He was considered the most strategic warrior everyone feared and depended on for security in attack times. He was expected to rule his people for as long as he was strong enough in his body to go to war in times of fierce battle.

Kingship also became an everlasting honor to the family/household from which the first King came. It was meant to memorialize the heroism of that person and his family.

It was inheritable, and the succession was always passed on to the first son (here again, not a girl child.) But the succession was transferrable to a brother next in line if ONLY there were no sons for the very old/dead King.

This made it another form of ownership in which leadership (the absolute power of decision-making) was assigned to only one man and his household.

So, on earth, the practice of paying homage to the King resulted in a rebirth, and the ownership of power brought the king a lot of riches. Local leaders appointed by the King to represent him in all places brought gold and all sorts of things to him. The way ancient kings obtained wealth can be seen in the story of the chief priest of my hometown.

In my maternal hometown, Putuken, River Gee County, Liberia, West Africa, the traditional ruler was called "Bodi-oh." He was confined to caring for the people's traditional things and was accorded the "Chief Priest" title at the advent of Christianity.

By the time I was born, my auntie had married the last Bodioh of my hometown as a second wife. I spent a lot of time with him, who was often addressed by his title plus name as Bodioh Nyensuah (Chief Priest Nyensuah). So, I saw a little bit of how things were done.

But the main point I want to make is that Bodioh didn't lack anything.

The lifestyle of a Bodioh was explained to me by my grandfather, who said before Bodioh Nyensuah took over, all those in the town, both old and young, had some form of responsibility to perform to ensure that the Bodioh didn't lack anything at all.

My grandfather said that all young girls were asked to fetch water and wood for the Priest's wives on a rotational basis, while boys had to bring in palm nuts used for making the traditional Grebo delicacy called "palm butter soup."

Yet, all grown-up men and women of the town had their own responsibility of making a farm for the Bodioh every year. In this process, the men brushed, fell trees, and cleaned the farmland while the women sowed rice seeds and all other crops and weeded and harvested the farm.

While the harvesting job was primarily the duty of

women, men also assisted in the process by handling certain aspects of the harvest work.

The men and women supplied fish and meat for soup kind.

His wives were considered Queen mothers who did not do any work but attended to the needs of the Bodioh, while he, too, had no other work but to attend to the needs of the Oracle.

My grandfather noted that former Chief Priests enjoyed such privileges until the advent of Christianity and National government systems.

Now, I was of age, and I noticed that under Bodioh Nyensuah, things were not done perfectly as my grandfather had told them. I remember that the town had a local representative for the national government who was accorded the title of town chief, thereby labeling the Bodioh as a traditional chief. Due to Christianity, the citizens were divided into two groups: those who said the chief priest represented evil and should not be attended to, and those who said tradition should still be preserved and could continue to make farms for him every year.

I also remember that Bodioh Nyensuah and his wives used to go to the farm to do farm work with our (the children who lived with them) assistance. But they didn't work too long, as right after a few weeks of starting any phase of the farm work, the town groups took their turns [men doing men's work and women doing women's work] to complete each phase of the job for him and his wives.

However, one important thing that didn't change when

Bodioh Nyensuah died without a successor was how to build a house for the Bodioh.

With my participation, while I was young, I saw that all boys and grown-up men were charged with the duty to build Bodioh's house in just one day while all mothers and grown-up daughters prepared food for the working men.

It was said that it was taboo for the Bodioh's house not to be completed in one day. Therefore, everybody worked from early morning until as late at night as it may have taken them to finish the house before midnight.

The Chief Priest ruled with a body. As Chief of the Oracle, who kept watch over the culture and traditions of the people, he was assisted by a group of elders whose responsibility was so complex and needless to explain in the context of a modern book. Earlier, his word was a decree.

The Bodioh title belonged to the "Syllapoe" family in Putuken. It was inherited throughout the ages, but it suffered continuity from Nyensuah's children, who refused to participate in ritual activities due to the advent of Christianity.

His central family line, the Syllapoe people, was the first family to produce the first pastor in the town who served the first church on our land. Pastor Jeddi, commonly referred to as Reverend Jeddi, was responsible for the conversion of many of his own people, including the sons of Bodioh Nyensuah, one of whom later served as the head pastor of the Faith Baptist Church in the town when I left Liberia in 2014.

One reason we find Spiritism all over the place now is this Grebo/Putuken scenario of abandonment. This is one topic to expand on during speaking events.

Chapter Seven

Different Knowledge (Human Science)

Still speaking of how ownership has negatively affected our world, let's see how human science divides us. But to do that, we have to return to the garden.

In the Garden of Eden, the Tree of Knowledge of Good and Evil contained the wisdom of God, which is the same He passed on to the angels. He said in Genesis 3:22, and it reads "And the Lord God said, 'The man has now become like one of **us**, knowing Good and Evil. He must not be allowed to reach out his hand and take also from the Tree of Life and eat and live forever.'"

Here, I want to explain the Good and Evil contained in this Tree of Knowledge. Firstly, let me say that God is the creator of all things. He owns them all, including the angels and us. As in the case of every owner, he/she has the right to do whatever he/she wants with the thing.

Now, God has the creative power [call it constructive power] and the destructive power [call it deconstructive power]. Therefore, He has the right to create for us all, and we will be pleased to receive, but when He breaks down what we have received, we think that it is bad, yet He breaks it down for His own good, not seeking permission from us. Even while we don't know that He broke it down to replace it with another one, we think that He has done a bad thing.

So, given the two sides of the coin; one, God breaks down for His own good and two, the angels or men think that what He did by breaking/taking away what they have received already is bad, the Spirit of God presents the Tree of Knowledge as good and evil (good from God's point of view and bad from servants' point of view.)

So, what is this Tree of Knowledge? The Tree of Knowledge is one of two important Trees [Tree of Knowledge and Tree of Life] in the Spirit Realm that contain powers from God.

The Tree of Knowledge contains good and evil [the knowledge {Science} of construction and destruction or simply put as to build and to breakdown] while the Tree of Life is the most sacred power that belongs to God alone.

Due to its sacredness, God chose to keep it away from mankind. Hear what He said to the angels after Lucifer had given the Tree of Knowledge to Adam and Eve, And the Lord God said,

'The man has now become like one of us, knowing good and evil. He must not be allowed to reach out his hand and take also from the tree of life and eat and live forever.'"

> — (Gen. 3:22 NIV).

See what God did after that, and it reads,

"After he drove the man out, he placed on the east side of the Garden of Eden cherubim and a flaming sword flashing back and forth to guard the way to the tree of life"

> — Gen. 3:24 NIV.

Note: Since that day, the Cherubs [Angels] have not left their guard posts.

The fact that the Tree of Life is nowhere to be found or seen on earth by human eyes proves that it is an invisible kind of tree that still stands in the place where the Spirit lives.

The Tree of Knowledge, therefore, contains all that God's power is, but right now, I'll focus on one, which is the power of making things, and in our world today, we call it "Science."

This power of making things (inventing) was passed on to man by Lucifer, and man (Adam and Eve) immediately obtained the idea of putting leaves together as clothes to cover themselves, just like Lucifer was covered with garments but real and beautiful ones.

So, the truth of the matter is that Lucifer [now Satan] was the angel of God who taught mankind how to make things. It can rightly be said [not gloriously] that he is the architect of human science even before God gave mankind the knowledge of science [for the sake of those who want to argue, let's remind ourselves of the sequence of the scriptures: Firstly, it was Lucifer who told them to eat the fruit of "good and evil." But before he did that, he told them that God knew that their eyes would open if they ate the fruit. Truly, their eyes opened, and they saw themselves naked/nude, which brought shame to them, and they rushed out to plug leaves from the trees and covered their nakedness/nudity even before God came. So, God came second to Lucifer when He (God) saw them naked and regretted the situation, so He gave them garments.]

The hidden theology the Spirit of God revealed to me about the episode is that God had the plan to give them the fruit of good and evil to open their eyes, but He is the God of time, so He was waiting for their maturity time. That's why He was angry with Lucifer for giving them the knowledge while they were not mature yet. God called it an impromptu action. The second hidden theology in the story is that the garments God gave at last represented the real knowledge of things for man, which means God fulfilled them at last after they had been exposed to science (creative art) already through the work of Lucifer.

Well, Lucifer [now we can start to call him Satan] had taken hold of human science. He would be dispensing it [giving it slowly by generations] to every human color or race.

So, as the King of the demons, he set in higher places to rule the human world, and he started dispensing [inspiring] human science throughout the world. This was seen as the knowledge every human race started developing to make things for themselves.

This made ancient black Africans make things for themselves, to heal and kill through the powers of the oracles. The ancient Chinese on their side did the same. The ancient Middle Eastern people, now called the Arabs, did the same. The ancient Europeans, now called the Westerners, did the same. Every other person around the world developed their own methods of making things. This is how Satan made science as universal as it should be, but he deviated from making it equitable along the way. Instead, he put more science in the hands of one race, and that is the white race. This means he dispensed knowledge faster among the white race more than he did to others.

The white race, among all human races, was chosen by Satan based on their color [this can be explained further in the other book titled *Interpretation Second*].

He chose them to lead (own) human science, and for this reason, the white people (Europeans) quickly began to advance their ideas of doing everything that man needs to do to make the world better or to make the world as beautiful as Heavens is. This made the white people the fastest thinkers, so much so that if they took knowledge from other people, they often developed it faster than the people they got it from.

Is there anyone to argue this? Well, start by asking yourself why the Western world leads the world. Why did they surpass everyone and eventually begin to imperialize their wills, culture, and traditions over all people through the trade of their artworks?

Today, they're the leaders in technology (Technical Knowledge), and from them, technology has spread to all nations.

Please don't say Americans are not Europeans, for we all know that Christopher Columbus (Italian) and Amerigo Vespucci (Italian) both came from Europe when they and early explorers stumbled over what was then called the "Newfound Land" while exploring the world around Europe, wherefore the newfound land was named after Amerigo as America.

The way Satan did it was the introduction of some things of God's rulership. He introduced democracy and capitalism [freedom to choose and ownership] to the Europeans. It was his way of using God's system of allowing the angels to choose certain things for themselves in Heaven, such as the right to choose what to eat. God called it self-willpower.

Also, he introduced to them God's system of owning everything that is in Heaven. So, the trick to look for things to own in the world is what he called *capitalism*.

These two systems of truth about God were exacerbated in the world to benefit him (Satan). Through them, he has the chance to control mankind and cause fighting over God's riches [fighting over natural resources]. Through these fighting, he would breed in wars [killings] to extract blood from the earth to keep his system alive.

So, the love of these two systems introduced to the entire world by Europeans has made them powerful because knowledge flows freely in democracy, and the game of seeking wealth is freely practiced in democracy.

So, they have been leading the world in everything until recently when other regions of the world began to copy their styles of doing things, and science began to blossom in those areas, too.

So, the idea of letting one human race have more knowledge in the world is satanic/selfish. It means having abundance comes with the spirit of pride. Pride is a little demon that dominates most people who are successful. Success is a word denoting having more than others according to our world order.

Unfortunately, what is Godly is not what the world knows much about. God's desire for humanity is a universal ownership system where everyone is equally served. This system received little attention in the world, which is why Christians don't know about it even while it existed in the life of the Christ Jesus everyone talks about every day.

So, you see, human science you see flourishing with the white man today was not meant to be so from the original plan of God, but such division caused among mankind by putting one above the other while God's natural resources are spread to all races throughout the world originated from the other heaven (another sphere called "Satan's Enclave.")

Two types of sciences

There are two types of sciences powering the human world. They are Spiritual and physical sciences.

1. *Spiritual science* – is the invisible power that makes human science works. It is responsible for creating and enabling human science work according to its desire.

Spiritual science is a force. It functions as human beings do when they create things and make them function the way they want them to function. This scenario explains that man makes a car, and he goes into the car to drive it to enable it to do the things it was designed to do. When this happens, then human beings become a force that creates and enables, just as every invisible force we cannot see does.

Since God created a bar between us and Him so that we cannot see Him, we think of spirits that we also call forces as different things more than we know ourselves to be living beings, but surely, they're living Beings like us.

In their world, they walk like us but in a different fashion. They have superior capabilities over us than we can imagine. In that world, a baby spirit is capable of lifting a thousand tons of heavy iron in our world unlike a thousand-year-old man. Unless they enable you to see or hear from them or see certain things in their world the way they want you to, you can never see or hear from them.

What is Sign?

Under this Spiritual Science topic, I will be discussing Signs. Signs are things that simply point us to probability, and probability is whether a particular thing will happen or has happened.

It is due to this concept of probability that certain things cause uncertainties in the eyes of mankind in Africa and the rest of the world. For example, before Christianity was born, ancient people, whether Jews or not, consulted mediums to solve mysteries. They would make a request for a child, for heroic power, healing power, and some other things simply by speaking out certain words or performing certain duties called "rituals," and thereafter, they got the reward just as they wanted it to be. And even now that Christianity exists against paying homage to these things, Christians still offer prayers to an unseen power, and they believe that that power can answer them according to their requests.

In fact, in the name of such power, other Christian groups perform rituals such as starving themselves for several days, and they call it "Fasting" to invoke the power of such force to earth to do what they want it (Him) to do. Now, when a desired response is given, we don't generally care to know how it is done, but we go rejoicing and praising the existence of whatever name we made our request to.

Therefore, I want to declare to you that those joys we share come from the signs we see through the receiving of what we requested. The signs (rewards) are the reasons behind our beliefs, and no one can easily dissuade us from what we enjoy.

So, we just learned and agreed that no matter where we find ourselves on the aisle, we all have one sense of supernatural existence called "Forces" (other living Beings). We also know that they're always willing to help us in creating what we want and how we want it. For that reason, no one can argue that there is a science (Power that creates) in the dark, a science that has all its factories and workers hidden from our eyes.

This type of science is called "Hidden Science" because it does not specialize in creating things directly in physical terms like we see scientists do. It rarely does, and when that happens, we call it "Magic/Make quick."

I'm a witness of magic in 2005. I will write about it in the future in a tract.

The word *magic* can be applied when things happen very instantly, unlike the usual. As in the case of instant healing. Magic also comes in when herbs (in modern science, we say "medicine/drugs"), which are physical things we can see and touch, are not applied to anything to produce healing or any other results.

Magic can also come when some other processes take a shorter time to do, like when spirituality was turned into physicality as quickly as possible when God dropped manna (food) from Heaven to the Jews in the wilderness. Magic was done when Jesus turned water into wine at a party. Magic was also done when physical objects (those staffs) turned into other physical but living things [those serpents in Pharaoh's Palace.]

Magic was acceptable in ancient times when sorcerers and sorceresses performed them to solve puzzles. And when

Jesus came, the people flocked behind him in large numbers due to his magical powers that surpassed all men and women of his contemporary time.

But today, it sounds very weird to talk about magic even though we still have them practiced in the traditional temples and in the Churches too. For example, people living in Africa are labeled with "African Signs," which is the best way of saying "Black Magic/Hidden Science." This means in Africa, people still go to the shrines [Visit the Sorcerers and Sorceresses] to ask for children, healing, and protection, and of course, they often succeed while at the same time, those who are said to have denounced the traditional things still go to the Churches for same reasons and they often succeed too.

The most important point to take is that all these powers belonged to the same source (God), except that satanic powers do not generally work in line with God's purpose, which is why they fall short of glorifying God. To glorify God means to make Him happy with you if you do anything that is in line with His will.

It is a fact in modern times that almost everybody belongs to a certain religious group in the world today. So, it is very simple to understand from the religious side the point that I'm making, just to get us to physical science. I'd like to use the Christian religion as an example.

In the Christian religion [the mere acceptance of things about the existence and power of God without/before physical proof]), prayers (Incantations) are offered on foods, water/liquids, and other touchable materials with the belief that God's Spirit would enter them to help carry on whatever is requested for. A prayer [incantation] could request God's blessings or protection.

That very thought [do this and let the spirit be the finisher] held within a religious cycle truly works in the science world.

In human science, man's duty is to simply obey and do what is required. The spirit could require any man to put physical materials together while the spirit completes the process to achieve the intended desire. How the process works is left with the spirit that gave the command.

This is what happens when someone wakes up one morning and feels a burning desire [a processing in the heart that is felt in the head] to do something. So, as he/she continues to focus (put all his/her heart) on that thing, he/she continues to receive impulses (messages) to lead him/her through a process that may result in the production (invention) of what came to the mind. The human mind is the exact processing point of the brain where the actions of the spirit are felt in one early morning or any other time of the day or night when the spirit enters the heart.

The "Information Superhighway" that represents Spiritual I-80

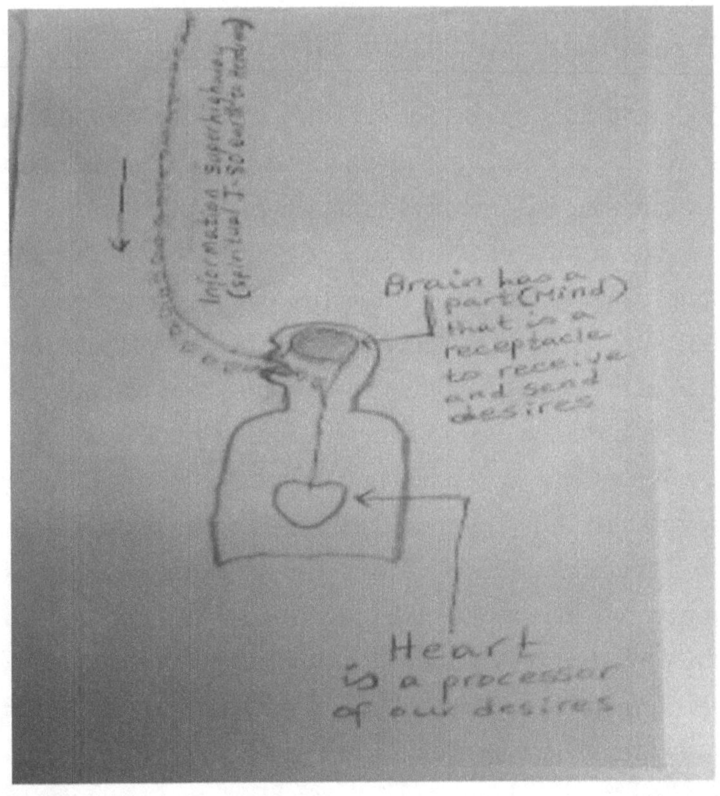

In science, if this happens, the scientist or person simply follows through with his/her instincts (impulses that keep falling on the mind) to establish a formula that leads to establishing something strange and new, but the mystery behind how the new thing functions is a work performed and enabled by something [a spirit] beyond the imagination of the maker.

"Cause Life" and "Blink Life"

Yet under this Spiritual Science study, there is one important secret about what goes on in the Spirit Realm before a human being is born unto his/her parents in our world.

This study will take us back to the Garden of Eden one more time, where God hid the Tree of Life from mankind, but He put the angels in charge of it because He said they (He and the angels) should not allow man to touch the Tree of Life so that he (man) will not live forever.

What this means is that God is the owner of the power or spirit called "Life," but the angels are the ones in charge of it.

Hahahaaaa!!! Earlier I told you to consider angels as robots or machines that God uses to do things He wants to do. You can also see that certain machines in our world today are responsible for carrying on other duties for other machines. For example, a truck is responsible for carrying/transporting heavy and light machines from one point to another, or a robot is used to feed or repair another robot. Even humans (God's earthly robots) work on humans.

So, if Life becomes one of God's forces/spirits that He put in the care of the angels, then it means the angels of God do know how to operate that machine even though they're not the maker and owner of it.

And, of course, Satan was once Lucifer, who was favored by God until his disobedience took him away. As we all know, his power was not taken from him. So, even while the Tree of Life was relocated to the east side of the garden, Satan had the ability to use it.

The fact that Satan's power of creation and every other

thing was not taken from him, he still could tamper with the Tree of Life [shake it] to squeeze out that power called "Life" to give it out to those who request children from his Kingdom.

The best and easiest way to understand this scenario is to quickly put your mind to how human science [communication technology] works in our world right now.

Nowadays, on TV and Radio, are news about one country or the other stealing information from another. In fact, militarily, when the next world war starts, other countries may not necessarily march infantry troops to their opponents to give them a punch in the eye or on the nose, but they could simply sit in their computer rooms to send powers of destruction to an opponent's country or to an individual person.

Every day, we hear about small wars such as Cyber Attacks. Through Cyber technology, information can be received or sent to another without seeking any permission.

This has just heightened between China and America as they begin a fight over who should be in control of telecommunications technology.

According to the CNBC's January 27, 2019 News report by Berkeley Lovelac Jr. under the caption *"Trump administration reportedly pushing allies to bar China's Huawei in race for 5G networking"*, means America got into a propaganda war against China by running a worldwide campaign to persuade other nations from buying new generation internet technology components from Chinese companies such as China's 5G company, Huawei. China's 5G is her next generation of ultra-high-speed internet.

The US accused the Asian tech giant country of espionage intent through internet tech by using low-price sales for tech materials to the world. Of course, espionage tactics are not unique to China alone but are a practice of all nations, including the US itself.

Now, this is a new kind of war about internet technology that best explains what happens in the Heavens. It means whoever wins the war of business to sell more internet components to Europe, Asia, and Africa will have the opportunity to carry on easy spying techniques on whatever the buying nation is.

But America already controls the world monetary system as well as exalting more military control over other nations, and this brings in China and Russia to find a way to reduce, if not eradicate, that monopoly of power, which explains why America is so fearful.

So, you can now see that countries are competing against one another because we have a world that is full of ownership system where people pride in what they have and fight to always defend it.

Had it been that both Communist/Socialist and Democratic ideas were blended by all.

peoples, and the world was with just one government like Heaven is; there wouldn't be need for one nation fearful of another, there wouldn't be fears of spying activities [for there will be one circuit for information gathering and dissemination as is in Heaven], there wouldn't be fear of facial recognition technology for that is how Heaven monitors every angel wherever and whenever it goes [for every day's news about these new technologies tells how the world is gradually growing towards how sophisticated heavenly science is such that information sharing {how fast forces (God's Spiritual workers) that carry voices and images travel from one point to another in their world (the air) in the forms that we call the waves; Radio and Electromagnetic waves, and others} as well as how fast the destructive agents we call missiles and their likes go to their target areas].

Similarly, like I always say, our world is a replica of the invisible world. So, Satan is that other country (but a sphere) in that invisible world that doesn't need the consent of God to do whatever he wants to, and the ability to steal/hijack Life from God's terrain doesn't require him to go there.

When he invokes Life (God's sacred power) to earth or into the womb of a woman, as when anyone visits the shrines to beg for the blessing of a child, it is called the "Cause of Life" in the Spirit World. It means that Satan or any of his demons have simply caused/triggered life to earth or to the womb, where the forces of formation are gathered from the sperm and the egg of a man and a woman to make a living being. The process is a Spiritual assembly requiring different resources (people, tools, and materials) for the work to go on.

Similarly, when God's believer goes to a pastor or prophet with a request to have a child, the angels in Heaven also shakeup/trigger the power of Life to descend to earth into the woman's womb and all the forces, tools and materials are assembled to form a living being in the womb of that woman.

Another thing that God holds sacred to Himself is Death, which is the opposite of creating living things. It is the ultimate power He has over the angels to destroy them whenever He wants to because He created them all. Perhaps these are the two most sacred powers of God that the angels of Heavens don't know how to make, but they can use them.

The way the angels/spirits use death is called "Blinking of Life." It is the way of squeezing Life out of a living thing. It is like what a human being does when he strangles an animal to death.

Because human beings do not see or touch Life in their fellow being or any other animal, out of their wish for death on another, they may perform any act of suffocation on the person or animal. They may also puncture the body by cutting or boring through it to let blood and water that cushion the body parts in place go out of the body to cause collision and rupture of several parts in the body, thereby leading to the outing of Life.

Likewise, the forces of God only torment/strain/stress life, and by this means, God is triggered to retrieve life out of a suffering man, and when this happens, the forces call it "Blink of life."

The word "Torment" is associated with all the forms of suffering that every man passes through till death. It includes nightmares that cause sicknesses as well as the struggle (convulsion) each dying person experiences.

This is a purely satanic form of blinking life. However, the word "Strain/Stress" is associated with the peaceful taking of life by the angels of God when a man has aged well to or little over 120 years.

Peaceful means of taking life are very unpopular in our world today since Satan's work has been the reason for short life spans, beginning with abortion and infant death.

2. *Physical science-* is when Spiritual (invisible) things turn into physical (Seeable and Touchable) things. It is the product of what has started in the Spirit Realm.

Physical Science is the real definition of God, which has two major parts; one part is the softest one that is not seeable and touchable. It is hidden inside a coveted (covered in many layers) world, and the second part is the hardest one that mankind can see and touch.

While the first part of God is very soft and easy to bend like the xylem of a plant [See Cassava plant], situated far inside the hardwood with many layers, the second part is very, very hard and difficult to bend or break.

So, you see, these two worlds (The world of the Spirit and the world of the human) work together to make everything that we have in this world possible. It means that God Himself is Science (A maker), and He passes on to [inspires] us, mankind, to do as He does and to be like Him.

So, He taught His angels to teach us what He knows and when they teach us, it is He who has taught us. Therefore, Science today comes from God, the maker of everything, regardless of which spirit inspires us. The only difference is the question of what the motive behind what the spirit has taught us is, is it evil or good?

Since the motive of Satan from the beginning was evil, meaning "Do wrong or go your own way," God had long ago sanctioned that no matter what he (Satan) does, it will never be acceptable until it is scrapped off and be replaced with what meets the general standard of all. That is why human science today shall be scrapped out at the end of time, no matter how beautiful and sophisticated scientists might go with their inventions.

No matter which bunkers a country's scientists build for the rich and no matter how far they go into Space establishment, everything belongs to God, so He shall scrap them off all to re-establish a world in which division and ownership shall have no place.

At the publishing of this book, God shall, by this means announce to the world's scientists that they shall begin to face battles in Space World where they think they can create a new place for human habitat.

Now, look at the first wrong thing Satan did to human science. He gave it to one humankind (white race) in abundance while he kept other races trailing behind them in the world. This has caused so much pain and heart hurting, as well as complaints in the world. The complaints in people's hearts are loud sounds in the Spirit realm. They cause disturbances similar to anyone causing nuisance in our community, which is why they would be charged with disturbance of public peace.

So, under this ownership system that Satan introduced to the world, one race is filled with pride and ego over all peoples and thus uses technology to suppress and subjugate other nations. The cries of the people are heard sorrowfully in Heaven.

And now that he (Satan) has decided to fulfill the part of another people [The semi-white race of the Middle Easterners and Asiatic Indians, including other white-color people of the Chinese and Russians class with non-democratic ideals] by giving them technological ideas, second to the European people; his dream of divide and rule has been achieved when we see anger, envy/jealousy and vengeance taking over other nations, all which are endangering the peaceful existence of humanity.

The second wrong thing Satan has done with this scientific knowledge is the misuse of death power, which operates several departments, one of which is the Department of Arms/weapons of destruction.

Speaking from the Spiritual point of view; weapons are

not evil but are tools used in the Spirit realm to puncture or dissolve the body to deflate it with life for certain reasons so that what should be done to the body can be done.

This is similar to an operator taking his vehicle to a tire shop for fixing, and the tire man's first duty is to deflate it with air before proper work can be done. In this way, deflating the tire is for a good purpose as opposed to anyone deflating another man's tire with the sole intent of impeding movement or causing other harm to the operator.

In the case of weapon, it is a terminology used to describe the largest tool often used to break down solid and elaborate structures in either a blasting/explosive manner or a dissolving manner to cut down time consumption if we had to use a bulldozer or other equipment. But if these weapons are used with the intent to take away life [another strangulating strategy to force God to take away Life power], then the purpose becomes evil.

So, you see how Satan has turned good into evil in the world from the scientific point of view. As we go further and further in this book, I will continue to give you more examples of how Satan has turned a lot of good things in Heaven into evil purposes in the human world, even while we tend to enjoy them for our own desires.

Not too long ago, I mentioned that other nations are expressing anger and frustration over the attitude of other people who first received an abundance of scientific knowledge and are using it to suppress and hold in bondage other nations' self-rights. This is the reason for terror suicide tactics in the world today, and the terrorists turn good things into weapons of mass destruction for themselves.

You know what I'm talking about when we hear news reports that a man or a woman uses her own vehicle to drive through a dense population of people to kill several of them even before someone kills him/her or still plunges into any building that he/she knows contains a crowd of people so that the vehicle would blast up into flame of fire to set the house at blaze and kill people while he/she dies with them.

Here, you can see that his/her own vehicle, which has been used for the good purpose of transportation all this while, has now been turned into a weapon of mass destruction, such a weapon that he/she needs to kill his/her suppressors or opponents but is difficult to obtain. So, terror groups are copiers of Satan's style of using good for evil for self-reason.

Chapter Eight

Marriage and Marriage Ring

Ummmm! Here, we are, again, going to the Garden to deliver on another form of ownership system peculiar to the human world alone.

So, for a refresh of mind, let's say that the Tree of Knowledge in the Garden of God contains scientific power (The power of making things as when Adam and Eve ate it, and they knew how to make clothes for themselves through the fig leaves to cover their nakedness.) But right now, please take a ride with me to another level. This means that besides the Tree of Life and probably Death, the Tree of Knowledge contains all that God knows and is the same as what He taught the angels to teach us. So, here I am to talk all about sex (System Extended Xebra; Xebra means "For energy.")

Firstly, I'll tell you whether there is sex in Heaven and, secondly, how sex is used for evil in the world of ours.

Yes, the word "Sex" exists in Heaven as every other word does on earth. But in Heaven, sex is a communication tool or a medium of power exchange. It is how power is transmitted from one source to another. God uses it to instantaneously communicate (Transmit) power to all His angels.

Just this month, October 2018, the US government set up a presidential alert system for President Donald Trump and all future Presidents of the United States to communicate with the entire nation through a single Text Message. That's the type of technology that best explains how God uses sex in Heaven.

Sex is sacred to God, but it is very different from how we do it on earth. So, be careful you don't confuse God's method with the way a man and a woman conduct sex together in our human world.

The next question is: do the angels marry since they can have sex? The answer is capital NO! Firstly, "Marriage" in Heaven means "Maturity Age." It means there is an age/stage that every new angel must reach to be able to do things for God, and when that time reaches, there is a training session that is conducted to teach or inspire the new angel with every activity carried on in Heaven.

So, sex is a communication process that is conducted by way of showing demos through videos as to how it is done.

Let me say it better: Sex training [a demonstration of the methods of passing on God's power/knowledge from one angel to another] in Heaven is done by showing the actions through a tech means called "Video" or "Visual Decode."

Quickly, let me say this: the practice of having sex in our world today using video is copied from Heaven to earth to be "Pornography." While it is a good thing to do for young couples, it is supposed to be restricted to grown-up men and women on the internet. There should be a tech means to block underage girls and boys from accessing it on the internet. Such unlimited access granted to all, regardless of age limit, is aimed at committing rape on kids.

Oh yes, rape was the act Satan carried on in the garden when he inspired Eve first [immature passing on of knowledge is to force an idea upon another]

Rape also is the act of making someone know sex prematurely, as in the case of an underage boy or girl, but sex forced upon someone and against the will of that person already with sex experience can be rape, as in the case of a husband to his wife.

Oh yes, Eve was yet immature according to God's set standard for man in the garden, but Lucifer tantalized her with the beauty of his garments, and he said to her, "You can get yourself out of nakedness if you should do this."

There, in the garden, Lucifer didn't enter Eve because he considered her filthy. But he showed her videos that demonstrated how sex (the passing on of the power and knowledge of God) should be while hoping that one day he would be able to enter her.

That day came later when demons began to seduce the daughters of men on earth (through sex dreams). When that happens to a young girl or boy who hasn't had physical sex, he or she automatically obtains the knowledge of sex. In the meantime, the demon (spirit being) has planted a seed of sexual desire inside the person's body.

Secondly, sex in Heaven is the free exchange of God's power/knowledge. So, marriage in Heaven is the maturity time for a new angel to experience the exchange process of God's power, while marriage is entirely different on earth.

On earth, marriage is a form of *ownership* [when men used women as their property in ancient times.] It is also a *business* or *trade* [when parents exchange their daughters for money in modern times]. See the title "*The Book of Interpretation Second*" under the topic "Marriage Today."

Back to how angels have sex. I tell you this: sex among the angels is not a vigorous type because the angels have no bones and muscles as we humans do. They're soft in body kind, so sex for them is a mere touch and a quick one at that [I recommend a video showing how two dragonflies can have sex in the field while flying.]

The flying dragonfly method demonstrates how an angel gives power while another receives power. The exact process is best explained by the jet-to-jet fuelling technology used in emergencies.

According to technology news I listened to one day while in the U.S., a flying jet plane may, for some reason, run short of gas [gas is a natural {God made} material that contains fire energy], so that another jet plane filled with gas may be sent from Air Base to fly in close range to the hungry plane and when the stomach-fill plane gets very close to the hungry one, it attaches a tube to the other, and pumps in the gas before it goes away after that.

This happens because there is energy (a power from

God) stored in liquids like gas and fuel that machineries need to continue to do their duties.

This plane-to-plane analogy tells you how angels get re-energized by a new one sent from home when the one losing energy has been involved in a battle with demons while flying through a sphere occupied by Satan's forces. This happens when an angel is sent to earth or travels back from earth to Heaven.

This fatigue and re-energizing scenario also explain what happened to Jesus when the Bible said Satan took him up to the Mountain to tempt him. What the Bible described as temptation was a Spiritual fight between the two, but Jesus was re-energized by a new power from Heaven to defeat Satan.

It wasn't easy at all for Jesus because he had lost some of his Spiritual capabilities once he became flesh, but his father (God in Heaven) had to send down more power to re-enforce him to overcome the Spirit (Satan.)

Chapter Nine

Marriage Ring

We have discussed what marriage is in Heaven. We said it is the maturity period when sex, which is the process of exchanging God's power, is taught to a new angel.

Also, we used the jet-to-jet analogy to explain how angels conduct sex clearly, but there is something we didn't mention. We didn't tell you how the angels wear rings on their fingers or toes as marks to indicate sizes.

Oh my God, this is ridiculous to talk about, but I must say it. The *Marriage Ring* [maturity mark] indicates size for sex and is often worn on different fingers or toes of all the angels to identify sizes. This means the finger or toe of a female angel on which a ring is worn indicates her size for the male angel that comes to her. It means a male angel with the same finger or toe and a ring on it is the perfect fit for that woman.

This happens in Heaven because God is a man of laws. Regardless of how elastic (malleable) the angels are, they're never allowed to mismatch one another.

But the ring method is what Satan has turned around once again in our human world. As for him, he introduced the marriage ring system to mankind as a sign of showing that a particular woman has been purchased for ownership by a specific man. Still, he refused to stick to the one big law of Heaven that ensures a woman's good health. He fools around to say that the woman's system is elastic so that it can afford any size, but the truth is that it leads to oversizing and sometimes tearing, causing impairments in some women.

Unfortunately, his agents responsible for sex fondling induce sexual cravings [body's itches for sex] in the world, so much so that many women think that oversized men are the best for them. Some women are unaware of its implications for their lives.

When I see them on social media bragging about how satisfying it was with him with that size, one thing that plays on my mind is the question of whether God didn't have the sizes of the other men among the men. I ask myself the question: are there no women in the world with the S & M sizes as the other women with XL sizes?

So, Satan uses this same mismatching method to cause sexual dissatisfaction in most marriages, mainly when a man or a woman has known another woman or man before meeting his/her wife/husband, or when he/she leaves his/her partner and goes cheating out there.

In addition to other topics, I will discuss under the Women of the World topic, I must emphasize that this mismatch of people today is one cause of marital infidelity.

The specific thing of the marriage ring

The Spirit of God gave me another scenario for re-energization in the Heavens. It was likened to a fuel station where vehicles go, and a hose with a nozzle is extended to its tank to empty gas or fuel into the vehicle. Fitting a nozzle into a hole at fuel stations is the exact use of a ring on angels in Heavens.

Since male angels are required to go to specified areas for services (cleaning and refilling), God marked their fingers' sizes by putting rings on their fingers as the female angels are marked on their fingers also.

So, a decree/law had been issued for everyone to obey. This means every male angel is bound to go to a female angel that wears a ring on the same finger as does the male angel. No mismatching. [Have you ever heard some women having more satisfaction with a certain size while others feel hurting with the same?]

However, from this practice of angelic women staying in one place to receive their male counterparts to service them comes into our world, another practice that many people of all levels have been enjoying. Let's see that later in what a brothel stands for.

Chapter Ten

So, why did God allow Marriage?

Unfortunately, Bible believers were not well informed by those early people who interpreted the mysterious book of Genesis. The book contains some statements of God's prediction of Satan's activities, compromise with Satan and mankind, frustration over their attitudes and behaviors, reluctance, and other things that are not God's true will. It means that God said certain things that were not His desire for the world; rather, the ways of Satan in the future.

One of such is the statement of,

"Therefore, a man shall leave his father and mother
and hold on to his wife, and they shall become one
flesh,"

— Old Testament

or

"That is why a man leaves his father and mother and
is united to his wife, and they become one flesh."

— NIV

Before I reveal the truth of the scripture, let's imagine the
different translations people offered, often paraphrasing
God's words in different ways over different periods.

So, what really happened? Let's start with what the
Christian Book says. It says God is All-Knowing. He knows
the future as well.

That makes it true that even before Lucifer rebelled
against God, God had already seen how Satan would teach
mankind how to own things, and he (Satan) would make a
man buy a woman, and it would be named marriage.

God couldn't have stopped it at the time for some reason,
so He predicted it.

What God saw and did was as when any nation's President
sees some dissidents planning to undermine his leadership,
but he had no means to stop them immediately because
it was difficult to get at them. So, the president would need
enough time to put resources together for the operation.

That was why He (God) announced that the man shall leave his father and mother to go unto the woman, and they shall become one as husband and wife. This announcement was made right after God had just made the woman, so He used a conjunctive adverb "Therefore" to start His announcement:

"Therefore, shall a man leave his father and his mother, and shall cleave unto his wife: and they shall be one flesh."

— (Gen. 2:24 KJV)

This, THEREFORE, was for the phrase BECAUSE I MADE WOMAN a man shall be bound to purchase a woman for a property in the Kingdom of Satan.

Did God really like the idea of a woman being owned, or did He like the whole idea of ownership thing by Satan and man? NO!!! Then why did He make the pronouncement?

Why didn't God stop Lucifer from going ahead?

So, there were two major reasons why God accepted [allowed] marriage to be. (1) Satan was still an important tool to use to complete His (God's) creation, and as such, it was too early to destroy Satan.

That's why Satan was still attending meetings in Heaven, and the Bible tells it as Job's Story. The Book of Job means "Job story" or "The job (work) you do." It means God saw this dissident child of His among the others and asked him how his job of deceiving and tormenting people in the world was going (Job 2:1 NKJV).

The point is that, if God had cut off every activity with Satan, then there was going to be no communication between Him and Satan after Satan was already cast down from Heaven. And (2), God needed to use the human body [Bible says God's Temple] for Himself, so He thought those who will yield to the call to marriage would be in a better position for Him (God) to use.

Virginity and faithfulness

So, God inserted His plan into Satan's plan of marriage. He introduced the virgin-before-marriage and remain-committed-to-one-after-marriage concepts.

How God uses those who obey the law of virginity before marriage and stay faithful to each other after marriage is detailed in Chapter Four. There, you would learn about why God is interested in human sex, which is why He demands that the body be kept clean for Him.

Chapter Eleven

Should everyone marry?

However, the idea of keeping human women in the houses for domestic chores as was done in ancient days was not anything wrong at all, for it worked alongside the heavenly practice of Spirit women receiving and taking care of their Spirit men after the men have returned from workplaces. The only wrong thing that was done was the level of abuse that was meted out against the human women.

Even now, if a man's earnings are enough to take care of every need for him and his family, so he decides to let his wife stay home, then fine, but not with the intent of abusing her.

An abuse to a woman comes in when she is denied free expression of her mind. She is abused when her needs are not attended to at the right time. She is abused when a man beats her, even in her own rights. She is abused when she is over-loaded with domestic chores that require assistance. She is abused when she is forced into her marital duty, even in her unhealthy condition. She is abused when she is not a friend but a tool that doesn't know rest. She is abused when anything unpleasant is directed towards her. And finally, a woman is abused when that which is not good for a man is done to her. I'm quite sure that when all these things are carefully observed, a man's wife shall never disrespect him.

Yet the Lord our God also requires an equal reciproca-tion from the woman towards her husband. Just as the husband shall remain faithful to his wife, so shall the wife be. The husband shall not come home late or give any excuse to his wife when, in truth, he has been with another woman. Likewise, the wife shall not abuse her going out and visiting friends and relatives for seeing another man. All rules must be observed by both parties, a peaceful home is theirs.

For those who shall choose not to marry, the Lord our God has this message for you. There shall be a thorough judgment on you on that day because you have chosen to starve the Lord God with hunger and thirst through the pollution of His temple.

Even while I came to the end of this topic, the Lord, God, Almighty, is asking me this question: Have the married ones obeyed the laws of marriage? Have they defiled their bodies as did the unmarried ones who go from one woman or man to another? He said, as far as He sees in the world, everyone has gone against the law. He said both, the married and unmarried, believer or non-believer, have been practicing promiscuity all over the land. That's why He is starving, and that's why He wants to end the system as soon as possible.

Chapter Twelve

Lesbian and Gay practices

Another way mankind has started to starve God is through using improper methods of having sex and for a recap; sex between a woman and a man is the proper method when they go natural so that a man's fluid is cooked well after squeezing through his tube to empty into a female's basin where a delicious meal is made for our heavenly father. See the *Interpretation Fourth* book for more information on sex.

Therefore, a healthy woman who decides to abstain from having a man shall be guilty of arbitrary (Illogical) refusal to perform her duty as a woman. She has thereby starved the Spirit of its desire. Likewise, a healthy man who decides to spill his semen into an undesirable vessel is guilty of the same crime as the woman.

I tell you this: it is an endorsement of sin for a couple to live apart from each other because of work or any other thing, for that matter. If this happens between two couples, it means that they have agreed or endorsed [unanimously] to engage in sexual sins by living far apart from each other because of work distance [Often, many couples live in different cities or countries]. It means that each partner is permitting the other [without admitting to the fact] to engage the services of a different man and woman for sex while staying away for more than a week.

Business travel or any other travel that is believed to last for more than one week should be taken together as a couple, except the two agree to abstain from sex for a certain amount of time, and this agreement must be adhered to by both sides (1 Corinthians 7:5 NKJV).

The purpose of avoiding a more extended stay apart is to avoid extafication. [Extafication is the swelling of cells with life in the body.] This is not good for the body.

The impact of extafication on the human body is felt in different ways. Firstly, it is the [most noticeable] craving desire for sex that every human feels at a certain point in time. Secondly, it [unknowingly] causes slumping, frequent hallucinations, etc., in others.

Extafication is a part of the sex system that certain spirits [demons] play with to increase sex desires in almost every human being in the world so that the constant supply of hormonal food can remain nonstop. It may also decrease below the expected set standard for a few people.

The tuning-up of extafication is a violation in the Spirit realm, as is tuning-up music in loud sound in our world of music, which the legal system calls "disturbance of public peace."

Chapter Thirteen

Amend Corporate Policies

As new as these rules may be, they may be of great help to our marriages if nations want to do the right things to save the world from Satan's domination.

Companies could change their employment policies that encourage marriages through a two-into-one employment base. This is when a husband and a wife seek employment in a company as one applicant. The two may be hired but not necessarily in the same department since they may have different skills and educational levels.

Parallel Marriage

To ensure proper employment entry into our advanced companies nowadays, education is a good recipe for this

process. That is, a marriage between educated and unedu-
cated individuals in today's world is unhealthy. [Education
herein refers to when a man or a woman has gone to school
to learn how to read, speak, and write correctly.]

Education is good for both a man and a woman to attain
various skills to use to get a job for the well-being of the
family (husband, wife, and child/children). Regardless of the
differences in education, the abilities to read, speak, and write
properly make a couple of Parallels, and it would help a long
way to move them forward in their search for a job.

Chapter Fourteen

Why should marriage bonds continue?

What should a husband or wife do if the other is sick enough and unable to flux the other's system? Well, this is automatically tantamount to death, and the other is supposedly not obligated to the sick. Out of goodwill (compassion and kindness), the healthy person may show care for the other. He or she is totally permitted to remarry, and the other may be taken to a folk home or any care center.

This law does not cover partial impairment, any impairment of any partner that doesn't stop him/her entirely from having sex.

Here is the case settlement: marriage is a bond between a woman and a man. The bond comes with its responsibilities, the primary being sexual responsibility, and the rest are secondary. This now brings us to a complete digestion of what sex stands for.

I mentioned earlier that the Spirit uses the human body to process physical materials (Plants, mammals, Fish, birds, and minerals). These materials are to be dissolved into the human body. After dissolving, their energy is extracted and stored in the blood, the brain, and bone, as well as in men's and women's fluids. After that, the carrier spirits come down to take it up to Heaven for food and other things. See the *Interpretation Fourth* book for the carrying of sexual fluids.

Now, while the Spirit may collect its food from a single person's blood, brain, and bone marrow, it doesn't simply take the semen or estrogen of a man or a woman, but rather, it takes the combination of the two for food. WHY? Because a man's semen must be ejected through his penis, and during that process of ejection, the semen undergoes heating and compression as the penis vibrates (reverberates), making the muscles in the penis squeeze out unwanted components out of the total fluid. It is after this process of [Cooking] the sperm that it is considered an acceptable product for the woman's use, which ends up in the preparation of a very healthy food for the Spirit.

It is due to this requirement that a man's sperm is not acceptable to be spilled out. This same law makes the use of Condoms a prohibition to God.

Parable of fruit-eating

While I was still considering the importance of divorce over a partner's inability to perform his/her duty, on December 2,

2018, the Spirit came down to give me the parable of fruit-eating.

In the parable, the man of God told me that we should be aware of keeping others with us in a marriage even if they're half rotten because there is always one side that is useful for use, yet if we carefully ignore the bad side, like when a man harvests fruits. The harvester shall only enjoy eating the well-ripe ones, but when his/her fruits turn to be one-sided rotten or one-sided infested, he/she will have to carefully cut off the rotten part to maintain the excellent side for eating. The man of God said that, like the fruits we put in different baskets, God has various categories of people in His vineyard. That means there are people infested with diseases by Satan but remain good at doing certain things for God or the other partner.

So, marriage has had its importance in the sight of God. Still, it was used consistently by men of all generations to abuse or suppress women, sometimes killing them for simple matters that a man needed to understand.

The women of the earth were sobbing and wetting the ground every day. Their voices were heard in Heaven by their fellow women, who were as spirits as Satan and his men. So, they chose to come down to earth to rescue the women of the earth, but something strange happened after their arrival. Let's see what happened.

Chapter Fifteen

The Women of the world

What moved women of the earth to action started with the spirit women; they (spirit women) probably were the most obedient spirits in Heaven when the male spirits under Satan fled to earth. The women were and are still confined to special places but rarely switched between places when necessary to carry on their duties.

If anyone closes his/her eyes to visualize their duties in Heaven, it wouldn't be far from the responsibilities of workers in a maintenance shop or garage. The duties of garage workers are to sit there and wait for operators to come in for services, and the maintenance guys provide those services. On the other hand, if you bring this system to the human level, it wouldn't look bad at all, for it has become another kind of job for a particular sect of people. There is no suppression or taking advantage of another. There is nothing about someone selling services and another buying services because there is no buying and selling in Heaven. Therefore, everything everyone does in Heaven is honorable as a responsibility to God, the owner of everything.

Name of the first woman who invaded the men

The Spirit women remained obedient to God until one saw the need for them (Women) to come down to earth to rescue the human women of the world, referred to as the women of the flesh. Today, I announce the name of this powerful and brave spirit woman as "Mobee Salabatees." She is now the Queen of the Coast, for she has captured all the world's coastal lines and taken over everything that flows as a liquid/fluid in the human world.

Mobee saw that the Spirit men who fell to the Earth long ago under the leadership of Satan have not been fair to the human women of the world. She saw and was annoyed by the way they (the men) treated women in the world; the Spirit men made human men marry human women as their property and treated them as nothing of any value. They silenced women from speaking their griefs, and they denied them whatever was due them [most times killing them for their entitlements.]

Mobee thought that human women needed freedom, so she pleaded with God about the matter. God, in turn, granted her more power than Satan received in the beginning when he was yet Lucifer.

Time has passed, like billions of years, and Heaven was more advanced than when everything started with Lucifer and a few other spirits of God, so Mobee was entitled to advanced power (Imagine the world of 2 B.C.E. and 1700C.E.).

Maybe, just maybe, God intentionally sneaked in Mobee to strike a balance between men and women in the world until He gets ready to end everything at His set time.

Mobee then came down as a visitor to Satan. Indeed, it was a memorable day in heaven [heaven here refers to the space Satan occupies called his Enclave] to have received a woman visitor from above since they (the Spirit men) had fallen to Earth. They, particularly Satan, saw her coming as a sign that women had now chosen to join them in a fight against God for self-independence. They didn't see themselves as being alone anymore.

Let me make it clear quickly: the men of Satan have been seeing women of the physical world but not women from the Spiritual world.

Spiritual women have the same supernatural powers as they do, unlike women of the physical world, who can be tampered with by them anyway.

So, they believed that there was an opportunity to use Spiritual women to achieve certain things in the world. They thought they could still use them the same way they're used in Heaven, but little did they know that that was about to change to their detriment.

You see, Spirit beings do not see in the hearts of their fellow spirit beings as they all do unto us, and likewise, we do not see in the hearts of our fellow humans. The only person who sees all our hearts is God, who made our hearts [both 'angels' and 'humans']. So, He alone knows our topmost secrets.

That explains why God knew whatever Satan or Mobee planned in their hearts even before each acted differently in the world from His ways. That further explains that He allowed them [not to His pleasure but out of no chance to change it immediately] to do whatever they were/are doing for a short while.

So, Mobee stayed with Satan and later became his wife, using her tactics to exploit him for his secrets in the world.

He was charmed by her beauty, too, and he adored her as his Queen, which he put as "Quttieentte" and interpreted as "My Heart" or "The woman of my heart," "the joy of my heart," and "the woman in whom I'm pleased."

Mmmmmm, in my home country, Liberia, there is this slogan "Blay-sees-Blay, Blay-gives-it," which is translated as "A well-dressed person sees another who is well dressed, and he/she condemns his/her look." This is further translated to mean that an exceptionally handsome Satan saw an extremely beautiful Mobee, and condemned himself by surrendering his all to the woman due to her beauty.

Whoops. His under-lieutenants gossiped about and mocked him, but they also envied him for being the only one with a Spiritual woman.

Mobee's cunning desire in the men's territory was well in place in all this mockery. She then embarked on an experimental mission. She threw herself at every lieutenant to win their hearts to gain access to their local territories. This gave her a clear view of everything that was happening in the world. Then she drew her working plan and went back home (to Heaven) to bring in four other women who would be deplored to the earth's four corners.

With their plans in mind and Mobee now sitting in Satan's Palace as the Queen Mother to all the dissident forces of women from Heaven, the four women started the tour of the earth's interior to identify specifics to report to Mobee. Their entries to every layer of the world followed the same pattern that Mobee applied to all the lieutenants, and they won the hearts of all the local chiefs.

Uh, they were also beautiful, so every local chief took it as an opportunity to bypass their heads and connect to Headquarters through them. Can someone imagine what is happening now and why it's happening? These women had the free flow between the layers (borders) of the earth as they were not accountable to anyone except to the Queen Mother, whom all the local chiefs had heard of but had not seen, so the local Chiefs foolishly thought a relationship with any one of the women was a conduit to sending messages to the President (Satan) through the first lady (Queen Mother.)

So, the women began a full-scale operation of a quasi-government system, which means they brought in an additional seven women who took positions alongside the men over the seven Continents of the world. Eventually, a flood of women began to fill the Air space hanging over the earth's Crust, and all the countries previously known as Kingdoms around the globe received appointments of female leaders to help care for the male leaders.

To the male leaders to whom these females went, it appeared to them like the King ["Akkwakba," this is what they call Satan, their King] had issued a decree for everyone to get married. Still, to the women themselves, they were rebel forces in disguise to the men. At the same time, they also operated as women leaders who would supervise local women leaders of the human world in the foreseeable future.

Now, with the appointment of the various women heads to all the Kingdoms of the earth at the time, a women's government was established. Still, the establishment of municipal leaderships like the city-to-city, town-to-town, and clan-to-clan was left.

Now, somebody may help me draw an Administrative Chart ranging from the Queen Mother at the top to her four assistants below, their seven assistants, and their country-to-country assistants, all of whom shall later be called Queen mothers in their localities.

Please let me remind you that these characters I'm discussing here are all Spiritual Forces that we know in our world as demons and agents of Satan operating from the Spirit Realm to do things with humans in the human world. This is a chronology of how all the evil we have in today's physical world got to be.

All of this took several hundred years to mature to the point where the women decided to leave the men, who had primarily been occupying the hills, mountains, trees, and rocks while using the water for pleasure.

So, the water used for pleasure for the men was chosen as the appropriate place for the women to dwell.

So, on one good afternoon, Mobee just packed off her things from the Palace and jumped into the Sea like Lightning, and gradually, the rest of the women followed. On that day, Aquebus (sometimes spelled "Akkuepus"), Satan's City, went very cold. It was like Satan himself had died, for he was nowhere to be found.

The Women's Kingdom took over the Sea Water and all other waters worldwide, including anything freely flowing as a liquid. This is what makes them present in all areas. They're the water spirits everywhere in the world, even in the pools where women and men swim to feel the pleasure of water. They're even in every kitchen sink where water flows, doing so many things to us everywhere around the world in different manners, just as I'll be pointing out one after another as we progress.

Chapter Sixteen

Two kinds of Women's Kingdom

These women came down with one big objective: to fight against the ways men have treated women in the world. However, when they began to interact with physical men in the world, they found something very interesting, and that is what led to a fight among them that brought upon them an internal division.

Two groups emerged from the conflict over what is right and not right. One group desired the body of men so much that it chose a Highline position against men to punish them. That group is what I'll call the **Draconian women. Still, its head has been labeled in the human world as the 666-woman, thus reflecting the understanding that there is one big woman of six hundred and sixty-six women demons, sitting in higher authority, waging a fierce warfare against men.** At the same time, the other group is the moderate women who choose to play their heavenly role while working peacefully with men to change their behaviors and attitudes in the world and appreciate women's roles in society.

The women's world also has all the science of manufacturing, as do men. They're responsible for everyday fashions that tickle the minds of all those gifted with a sense of beauty. They enslave people to beauty, and the people buy and buy and buy so much that money has become the biggest idol of worship in modern times.

Generally, all the Spirit women are sophisticated, learning and doing many things. Sometimes, it is argued in Heavens that women know more than men or that men are more than women, but indeed, this is hard to determine since they're all involved in the science of technology now. However, one thing that is unique about women is their introduction of hydro technology [the use of water in technology, particularly hydroelectricity]. They're also credited for introducing the hydraulic system in modern science today.

The Two Together

Now add physical [earthly] women. With the help of METONYMY, we can now start to see these characters as either spirits or humans since the spirits manifest on physical earth through humans to do their works. It means that the Spirit women stick inside physical women to make the physical women behave the way the world sees them. So, when it happens, no one knows that women's behaviors are driven by invisible forces lurking within them. It is the same pattern as

Spiritual men to physical men when physical men pose themselves as the lords over physical women.

Only spiritual people understand how Spiritual beings stick inside our bodies, but I'll try to simplify it again by using technology.

Let's say we (human beings) can make things and use them to our advantage. For example, a man makes a car and enters the vehicle to operate it how he wants it. The man also makes a musical instrument and operates it how he wants it. While using his instrument, he has a way to adjust its sound system, whether it is higher or lower. When we (human beings) see the Spirit like us, we'll have no reason to argue how the Spirit can come into our bodies [full of holes or compartments] to operate it just as we do to our vehicles.

We can easily understand how spirit beings enter us and sit in there and operate our system to do those things they want to do when we see ourselves lying inside a box to cover ourselves so that no one sees us from a distance while we do something inside. We can also see how the same spirit uses us to make every sound that we make, whether it be talking, singing, crying, whispering, or yelling, when we see ourselves using Mics as our creations to make sounds, just as we are creations, too, for the Spirits.

I'm sorry. Even if I were to demonstrate in front of any audience how all this happens, you wouldn't understand it since you can never have the opportunity to see them entering and coming out of me one after the other to perform different tasks on my body, which is to them a complex machine that produces sound while lifting things, emitting lights, moving, cleaning some parts of itself at the same time, and so on. Isn't it wonderful?

In the EXTRAS section of this book, I provided some examples of how the Spirits enter our bodies.

The underlying point is that whether you see these characters as Spiritual (Invisible) Forces or human beings, you're just saying the same thing because these Forces drive human beings to do whatever they (human beings) do, so there is no way to separate them. The Spirit comes into a body (its machine) to do its work, and the only thing we see doing the thing is a human being, so we have all right to leave out the Spirit to say it's the human being who has done the thing, this is metonymy. Therefore, take me as the author of these stories, but I, for one, will tell you that I'm not the author but the one who uses me.

Since the human body is a complex machine [the combination of different types of machines], different operators come to work each moment of a man's life. So, the spirits come in and go out in a continuous (nonstop) style, which explains our breathing system.

Our breathing system is the up-and-down (in-and-out) movement that we cannot see. They keep changing shifts [going in and out] throughout a man's life until that person dies.

Moderate Women

This is actually a small group of women. They're commonly referred to as the Women's Rights group, which introduced the women's movements in the world. They started with women in the Bible whose love for Christ showed how essential women were in ancient societies (John 4:5-28, Matthew 27:55 NKJV).

They argue with men that women can be what men are and they can also do what men can.

They hold church positions, take up administrative jobs, and have technical careers among men. They are humble, kind, submissive, and respectful. If they were not bothered one way or the other, they would make perfect housewives.

Have you noticed some women in our societies who are obedient to men, who tell other women that men are the heads and must be respected, while other women say otherwise, that women have the same rights as men, so the respect must be reciprocal? When you see this happening, remember that both women have two different Spiritual women dwelling in them.

The woman who says men are the heads is the woman who recognizes how men were the first to start everything that exists today, beginning with God [a man], who created everything and ending with the Spiritual men who set up the system we have in our human world as cultures and traditions.

The moderate women are among the forces that convert people from sinful acts to righteousness. This explains why some people [be women or men] at certain points in their lives, regardless of who they are, become spiritual converts who administer healing powers, prophesy, speak in tongues, and other things in the Spirit.

The purpose of this act is to use a particular person who is so knowledgeable [maybe having been a prostitute or a drug addict or any bad character] to advise others to come back from that world, for it leads to destruction.

They have science, but it's very confusing. It seems evil, but it's good because its objective is to keep people married and obedient to God. [We shall find out later.]

The Draconian Women

Ummmmmmm, believe me; you wouldn't want to hear their stories, but calm down. Don't panic if you're a woman, no, no, don't be at all because these women are not working with women alone; they also work with men in diverse ways.

For the sake of not resounding the label "666" all the time, let me use the word "Draconian (ruthless)" for this group of women.

So, the draconian group hijacked men in the world; they are fond of treating men as rags. They have no mercy on any man; they plunder whatever men boast of through their sex fondling.

Evidence of Draconian women on earth

They poured out into the world to set up means of earning money for women. This was their way of bringing freedom to human women, whom human men often abuse and starve.

As ancient history showed, a goddess in ancient Mesopotamia called "Ishtar" captured men's services, thus setting the stage for how women use their bodies to make money for themselves to avoid waiting for men to provide their source of livelihood. This practice became known in our world today as "Prostitution," the practice of purposefully having sex with a man for something you lack. Let's hear the story:

Wherever we find evidence of human culture, we find evidence of prostitution. When the earliest known human societies emerged in the fertile crescent of Mesopotamia, the sex trade evolved alongside temples, customs, markets, and laws.

Beginning in the third millennium B.C., the Sumerians, the first major inhabitants of ancient Mesopotamia, worshipped the goddess **Ishtar**. This deity remained constant throughout Mesopotamia's Babylonian and Assyrian empires.

Ishtar was the goddess of love and war, symbolized by the planet Venus. She was born anew as a maiden every morning only to become a 'whore' every evening – the etymology of the word lying in the Indo-European root meaning 'desire.'

Ironically, Mesopotamian religious practices gave birth to the prostitution trade, as women in Ishtar's service would help men who offered money to her temples with the 'sacred' powers of their bodies. Only women who achieved a priority of communication with the goddess from their fertility enjoyed this religious position. Thus, Ishtar temples became knowledge centers concerning birth, birth control, and sexuality. Priestesses became the nurses and sacred sex therapists of these early societies. Men of all ranks could hire these women and, in turn, make an offering to the goddess from whose temple the prostitute came.

The king would also participate in certain sacred sex rituals with the high priestesses in conjunction with grain harvests: the fertility of the earth was secured through a ritual that celebrated the fertility of the womb.

The king, regent of the earth, and priestess, regent of the goddess, coupled in this highly symbolic manner, celebrating the sexual process that brought grain and people into being.

Thus, Ishtar became known as the protector of all prostitutes. Prostitution, or at least the religious prostitution involved in these sacred sex rituals, existed without taboo or prohibition.

Therefore, whether Prostitution is biblical or worldly, it has its roots in women's rebellions against men's suppression, and it represents their way of control and conquest of men.

With this history I uncovered during my Google search in 2018 of a goddess pouring out prostitution, I realized how concrete and reliable the information I received between 2006 and 2008 has been for me. I'm confident that the revelations I received on the emergence of women in power are not fiction and should not be treated as such.

Likewise, I believe another piece of revelation that says both man and woman were created at the same time, Male and Female (Gen. 1:27), but God did not start to use the two people at once; instead, He put the male to work first as indicated by the second creation of the man, Gen.2:7 then followed by the female, Gen.2:21-22.

So, the woman was brought to the man (Gen. 2:22) later while the man was at work. This pattern explains that the man is the head [first] of the house. It also explains why men initiated everything, and women's initiatives came second to men's today.

Wait, wait; something in Ishtar's history says about powers and communication in sex: "As women in Ishtar's service would help men who offered money to her temples with the 'sacred' *powers* of their bodies, achieving a priority of *communication* with the goddess from their fertility." Let's remember this.

Chapter Seventeen

What does Brothel stand for?

I hope you haven't forgotten that angelic women go to a specific place in Heaven to receive their male counterparts for service work. Still, now I say this: this system of male angels going to specific areas for services herein described as "System Extended Xebra (Sex)," has been introduced by the Spirit women as the "Brothel" or "Bordello" and several other names like "Massage Parlors," "Parlors," "Bars," "Strip Clubs," "Body Rub Parlours," "Studios," and so on where men often go to engage the services of women for sex but the kind of sex that men bargain prices for.

And yet the system of calling on one angel to the field for emergency filling has come down to earth as a travel partnership under which most men [of course, some women do too] often leave their spouses behind rather than spending the same money to travel with them but engage the services of other women during their trips away from home. Such travel partners, as women, don't necessarily have to station at public places like the brothel to be hired. Still, they come from all walks of life, such as married women and professional women, who some rich and powerful men take to travel with them during their travel journeys.

So, the payment of money by men to women on earth for sex is such a contradiction that comes in the offering of sex services. It explains how the selling and buying system explains the lifestyles people living under Satan's regime are subjected to.

Now, that brings us to narrow down the duties angelic women perform in Heavens. And I say, absolutely nothing except to wallope man. "Wallope" means to clean. It means the work of female angels in the Heavens is only to clean male angels after the male angels have returned from the fields of work.

That also means all the works in Heavens are done by the males, so after work (like when a machine has worked so hard), a man has to go for service and change other parts. So, one of those services performed is to extend God's power to the male angels, a process I laid out long ago, but for reminder purposes, it's called "**S**ystem **E**xtended **X**ebra (Sex)." If you've forgotten what Xebra means, it means "For energy." That means when we have sex, we exchange God's powers (evil or good) deposited in each of us.

But the place where these powers are scooped is the female reservoir. That's why female angels are stationed in one place where male angels go regularly to change their worn-out systems.

This is supposed to be the same on earth [remember the Lord's Prayer says, pray so that that which is done in Heavens shall be done on earth], but Satan's system of give-something-to-get-something has polluted heavenly lifestyles, but this would be for a while.

The best way to recognize these powers that we exchange is in two ways: (1) when they become harmful (disruptive) to the body, science will name them in several ways as viruses or sexual diseases, and (2) when a man pours in his Semen (transfer of man's fluid) into a woman's basin where a Spiritual mixture takes place to form a new human being.

Another positive effect of sex on the human body other than making children is body maintenance. This may not be visible to man's eyes as it occurs inside the human body. It means that when a man and a woman have sex, they help to flux (get rid of) some systems through the heavy pour out (breathing) of air done mainly through their noses and mouths as well as transporting other things through other pores (openings) on their bodies.

When some cells in the body are deflated (air removed), new powers are inflated (air implanted) in us for new duties.

Since sex is primarily meant for fluxing out air from the body to refill with new air power, it is not intended for a game where people compete for rewards, which may force them into having restless practices.

Sex should be carried on regularly but like once a day, depending on what activities a particular man does. This means a man who works one job and stays home until the next day should have his wife one time after he has arrived home and rested for a bit of time. His wife needs to attend to him without delays so that he may have a nice rest when the spirits to work on his body come into his body for repairs and renewal. But if he has some other work done after having sex, then he will need another flux out at the end before sleep.

Now technology is coming in to make most work easier; less energy and less time for a man to do a particular piece of job, he will need one-time sex as opposed to a man who had worked long in the factory where he lifted and carried heavy loads. That factory worker would need about two-time fluxing before going to do another job the next day. The two fluxes shall not be done intermittently (right after the other) but rather spread over a few hours. Preferably, he needs one as soon as he gets home, and he needs another before a full night's sleep. The purpose is to do a thorough fluxing, just like washing dirt off an object in two different liquids, to ensure that all dirt particles are removed.

LET ME EMPHASIZE THIS BUT NOT A SUIT-ABLE CONDITION FOR OUR PRESENT WORLD SYSTEM. A woman's duty is not to work but to care for the man (Titus 2:5 NKJV).

The kind of care she gives him is entirely, so to speak, wallope or bedwork. In addition to bed work, she has to breastfeed and feed a baby, if there is any. The man must do all other things. He may request free services or hire the services of other men to do the house chores while his wife rests in bed waiting for him to come home.

Hey, I'm not saying a woman doesn't need to go out to visit friends or relatives while her husband is out for work, but she must remember her duty to her husband when he returns.

How much sex [energy] each man needs [God's proposed standard] depends on how much work a man performs within a given period because a man working long hours and complex tasks needs a whole night's sleep, but a man performing less energy-consuming duties can sleep in the daytime if he wishes. The reason is that there are Special Forces for the body repairs that are made for the night, and the best time they travel down to earth to work effectively is when night falls, at which time human beings need to sleep.

Sleep is a condition every human being must satisfy to allow those quiet Night Forces to get to work. Has anyone wondered why sick people usually scream or feel excruciating at night falls? This happens when these Special Forces come down to work, and in most cases, they battle with other evil forces like Mr. Death.

Sex position: The most appropriate sex positions are just two and necessary for various reasons. The man who works long hours under challenging conditions gets home extremely tired. He needs sex, but his wife should be ready to give it to him while he relaxes. So, he needs to be in the under position while the man working easy jobs takes the reverse. Any other position, whoever practices today, is a fantasy created by the Women's Kingdom in their sex game.

Also, the Women's Kingdom introduced other games such as mouth sex, anus sex, etc.

The older man needs the under position. That's why an able woman is good for him, and this justifies the need for a man to marry a woman below his age. It is not an abuse to any woman younger than her husband, and since women have chosen to work equally to men in today's world, then when the husband of a woman dies, she is allowed as a wise thing to remarry a man below her age if she so desires.

Given that the original plan was for a woman to serve a man and not to work, a younger woman for an older man justifies her ability to do her duty properly. The same could have thrown the need for younger men to older women under the bus today, but that is no longer necessary since women have chosen to work equally to men. The reverse is a new code of law placed under the women's code of engagement, the school of equal rights.

Their arrival to earth brought new ways of life in a world that men started to rule as custodians of the law, but their own pomposity has moved women to action to ruin them off the things they own in this world [Let's have more on the women later]

Chapter Eighteen

Topmost secret of virginity and faithfulness

In chapter one, I revealed that God accepted marriage under Satan's buying and selling system of things in the world for two purposes, but one is to avoid starving God through the pollution of the human body. The pollution God was talking about is the transfer (communication) of maggots (satanic powers) like those from Ishtar.

What is satanic maggot?

When Satan and his men fell from heaven, they remained the children of God, but the bad ones He called "Maggots."

Since the human body remains a public facility for the Spirit, it means Satan and his collaborators also have access to the human body, but God looks at them as disruptive forces (criminals) who dine with the honorable men and women in the same public place. He thinks there is a way to minimize the level of damage they could cause in there, so He accepted men and women to remain virgins before marriage and remain committed to each other after marriage.

God's reason behind this theory is that a human being is a machine required to process the resources (plants, mammals, birds, fishes, and minerals) of the earth in the human body, and then the Spirit comes to feed and take supplies to Heavens for the nourishment of heavenly forces including God Himself. This means that when we harvest these things and eat them, and they dissolve into our bloodstreams, the angels [that include the good and bad] come into our bodies to feed and take some to Heavens, to God and all the other spirits.

The topmost secret that God has permitted me to share now is that His food comes from the mixture of man's fluid and woman's fluid, which are brought together through sexual intercourse. These fluids (Male's Semen and Female's Egg) are the cleanest body fluids that contain the richest food content for the Spirit.

That's why they must be preserved for Him, at least, in the holiest manner ever known, and the ONLY MEANS ever required is virginity (keep them untouched) until marriage, then keep them stable (commit to only one) after marriage.

Telecom Tower with her

The reasons why a man and a woman should keep to each other forever have long been stated, but let me repeat them in a precise way: Apart from the angels that enter the human body, there are different kinds of forces competing over control of the same body, ranging from the two great satanic kingdoms of men and women to the various classes of each Kingdom as a show of their internal divisions. So, the best and most powerful way these spirits move from one human being to another is through sex.

Sex initiation [the planting of an antenna in any human body] is a very powerful way of reaching the soul (the spirit part of man to which a spirit connects.)

Apart from what we learned about in the story of Ishtar; spiritual initiations are still going on in the world. It happens that some people are easily conquered by witches and wizards through sex contact. When a witch or wizard has sex with a freeborn (one without such different spirit), the demons in such a person are transmitted to the free-born, and after time, the freeborn begins to have some nightmares that he/she has not had before. This spiritual connection aids the spirit world to do whatever it wants to do to the person.

The initial planting of the seeds of witches through sex is like what science does when it first has to plant a communication tower in a particular locality before sending signals to that place.

This system of planting spiritual seeds through sex is not limited to witches and wizards. It is also found in the Church cycle. It helps to spread spiritual seeds by which a lot of people are entrapped by Spiritual healers in Churches. This means a prophet or prophetess who keeps on having sex with different women or men is knowingly or unknowingly planting seeds in them that they, too, transmit to others as long as they continue to have sex around.

Now this prophetic seeding thing helps to make people experience different levels of spiritual problems that require prophetic healing works as well as the uplifting of the Church.

In some people with less power of God [science says "Less Resistance"], those seeds turn them sick enough due to sins in them that they are often taken to spiritual healing centers, while in some people with different desires for God, the seeds help to grow the Spirit of God in them to become singers and praisers of God and, in some, the gifts of teaching, preaching, counseling, prophesying and healings are empowered.

In developed Countries, these spiritual problems are tackled with a medical approach and are therefore given medical names like "Mentally deranged" and other conditions that continue to persist despite medical treatments.

It will be shocking to know that in Africa, where prophetic Churches are growing in number day by day, spiritual problems are very prevalent. This is happening because other than sex implantation, the very Churches offer several powers to people through physical materials like bread, water, coconut, cassava, banana, olive oil, and any oil, soda (Soft Drink), and so on when they invoke certain spirits [some are false spirits from the marine world or a good Spirit on a special mission for God] in them through incantations ("prayers.")

This is another way of evading sex, which means reaching out to people of all ages, and it happens when people take these specially prepared materials to their homes where they don't eat or drink them alone. Instead, they often share them with their family members and friends, who then get captured by these forces depending on each person's body resistance (the amount of power of God present in a person.)

In the case of evil implantations, the power of God can always help to neutralize or destroy some of them only when the person has stopped visiting over and over the same church of an evil prophet/prophetess. Going to such a temple to keep on taking in these spiritually prepared materials turns the person into a captive of such power. This is the evidence when the person continues to report different spiritual issues to the prophet/prophetess all the time.

The issue of Spirituality is so complex that it is difficult for the human mind to grasp very easily, for what seems ugly may be the right thing at times. This happens when the same evil Spirit gives someone the gift of singing and dancing to use for exaltations and other purposes. I'm talking about a person who has been in the world of music for secular purposes and has turned gospel overnight or the other way around. This happens when an individual has begun to make use of his/her Will-Power by focusing his/her heart on a different thing, maybe as a result of an outside influence which compels the spirit in him/her to manage with him/her. And when this turnaround takes place, then people say it doesn't matter where he/she comes from as long as the talent has been used to praise God, but such utterance simply acknowledges the fact that all the Spirits do worship God, which is the sum of saying they all possess the power of God in them to sing and make music.

Each of these forces has its own magnitude of control over the body. In fact, their level of control over a person depends on their geographical origin. So, when a man has sex with another woman, there is an exchange of powers between them, and that chain of losing and gaining different powers continues with every individual who keeps meeting different people all the time. This process keeps the well of food shaky for God [I recommend a video showing how maggots perforate a pile of poop or a piece of decayed meat or fish.]

Each time His angel comes to dip into the well for the Master's food, the well turns muddy and unhealthy to take food for Him.

Those who live in the Western world do understand the transfer of powers through sex when science speaks to them about sexual diseases, while those in primitive communities do have the scientific understanding from the clinics they go to, but this is done along with their traditional understanding of witchcraft initiations through sex while those in the religious world also understand cultic initiations through sex rituals.

So, you see, we all have an idea of what the transfer of powers through sex means, so it's not time to overlook what this book is exploring in detail for you here. No matter which side you find yourself on, God is speaking to you today because this is his last message to begin the process of judgment for the people.

Chapter Nineteen

The power of the human body

The draconian women fell in love with having sex with the men of the world after they came down from Heavens, so they decided to use sex power throughout the world to exert their total control over men. But how exactly does a spirit have sex with a physical man?

Well, this is done in two ways; firstly, the spirit does this with a man's soul since the soul is every man's spiritual makeup [a representative of the physical body in the Spirit Realm] that operates in two ways like a body of water that stays running or stilt but evaporates in the air at the same time with a name change as vapor.

Like the water stays running and turns into vapor then, later condenses to become droplets of rainwater that return to the river, the soul also stays locked inside the human body while it flies into the air as a spirit (Air is the Spirit World), then later manifests back into the human body. This means that the soul turns into a spirit to do other things, and when it does so, it encounters other spirits.

During this period, the draconian women interact with the soul and may probably have sex with it, which is communicated back to the physical body as a dream in which a man sees himself having sex with a woman in his sleep or a woman having sex with a man in her sleep.

The purpose of this kind of sex with a human's spirit is to capture him/her permanently for everyday use.

In technology, this is called capturing signal. For example, when a new radio station is established, every man who wants to listen to programs on that station must first look for that radio station's signal or frequency on which it broadcasts or sends messages. Without capturing or locating its frequency (its wave system), no one shall have access to its activities.

This is exactly what happens to a man's soul when it goes on tour while the person is asleep. In that state of its touring the Spirit Realm, it participates in so many activities there; in some cases, it flies, it swims, it has dinner with others, it fights battles, it conquers or may be conquered, and, in all these, it continues to send signals to the human body that is lying in bed so that the person experiences any one of these activities in the form of a dream or "derama," a word which means to the spirits as "participation."

Chapter Twenty

Man's search engine

So, we have been talking about having time with a woman and the role of the spirits. So, let's talk about the role we play in all this, too, such as: can we be able to avoid these spirits or not, and if so, how?

This brings us to the heart that God gave us, which in this book has been described as the 'search engine of human beings.'

But to start with, let's find out what the Bible advises about the heart. Let me take just one example:

"Above all else, guard your heart, for everything you
do flows from it"

— (Prov.4:23)

However, the Bible doesn't tell us all the details about the powerful role that our heart plays. If it did, ok, but permit me to add emphasis to whatever is written about the human heart.

Now, I tell you this, the heart is our search engine. We use it just as we use the computer mouse to click on icons that represent certain activities, and when we click on an icon, we have just activated/triggered a power to action. How this happens in the human body is a coordination between the brain and the heart; the heart initiates desire and sends it to [clicks on] the brain, then the brain sends to [clicks on] the Spirit Realm whatever the heart desires there so that that thing, often in the form of a spirit, comes down and enters the heart through the brain. Some of it [the spirit] may enter through the mouth as well, which we feel as a breathing system.

This is why the desire to bring down the spirit of sex or reject it depends on one's search engine, the heart.

Now, take this scenario: there is a time you look at a very beautiful woman, and your heart begins to pound inside you, which is a growing of that desire, and the longer you keep looking at her, the more you get filled with the spirit of sex desire to have her and I bet you as a man, there is a swelling going on inside there, but as soon as you remove your eyes from her, there comes a heavy outpour of breath which is the returning of that spirit that was taking control of that whole body. When this happens, the man sighs a long breath and says, oh gosh, what have I been thinking? I got carried away by that lady. Women do the same, too, anyway.

So, a draconian woman that loves sex so much and

controls sensuality [herein means love of beauty] will fly down into the heart and continue to tickle it, and because you're so idle, having nothing to do, you begin to focus all your mind [clicking and clicking into the Spirit Realm] on which woman to grab and when you succeed, that spirit of sensuality begins to reveal to you all that you need to do such as; find somewhere cool to take her for good food [sense of beauty], nice and quiet environment to talk her into everything that is popping up into that mind from that heart and finally, getting her down for all the fun that the spirit is inspiring in that heart, is all that occupies that empty body. And they call it the enjoyment of the world [taking a woman out to beautiful places and eating and drinking and having multiple time is all they {draconians} called "enjoyment of the world.}]

So, when the time comes to put in action all the thoughts of the heart, the spirit [whether a draconian or any other] lies inside (align itself with) every human body to cause every sex action that a man or woman thinks about performing but the heart of a man is the search engine used throughout the process; that is, as soon as the person's heart goes to what to do or what position to take, whichever spirit that is responsible for that act responds to it immediately and when they're changing shifts, we as human beings tend to breath out heavily while sweating and sometimes airing underneath.

Now, when we are performing these actions for a very long time, we tend to increase the intensity of heat in our bodies, which is why these water spirits [living in cold water] come to us to heat their bodies.

They like it so well that they would never want us to

stop, so they have to give us the strength and desire to continue to have sex almost nonstop.

They change shifts one after another to warm themselves, and we're like a beach on which they sun dry themselves. This is where the sexual sins that a man (male or female) commits come from when he/she is not able to find his/her partner ready to have sex at the time his/her engine is turned on.

The turn-on of the search engine

The turning on of a man's search engine is called "Fondling" which is controlled by the Spirit. So, as the spirit continues to want you to warm or feed it, that's how you continue to feel the desire for sex, and for some people, they wouldn't hesitate but rather put their minds to it, helping the spirit to take full control of the man's body until he/she has had sex with anyone willing to give it as well.

Every male and female has the ability to reject such unnecessary demands for heating the spirit, but unfortunately, not many people are ready to keep on rejecting these constant demands, particularly from the water spirits.

The way to reject sexual urges is by taking your mind out of it and having something to occupy your mind, and avoiding close contact with the opposite sex, particularly in lonely places where your attention will be captured very easily.

The idea of preoccupying your mind is always rooted in God's call for Christian assembly. The need to help each other to get the minds occupied all the time supersedes the belief that praying sincerely to God in one's own heart without mingling is enough to worship God.

Uses of Hypnotizers

Another big reason why the water spirits use the body regularly is to ensure that the rich food supply obtained from the human fluids does not stop going on night in and night out. This third reason is behind the introduction of hypnotizers [drugs {tobacco, cocaine & their accessories}, alcohol, and pharmaceuticals] so that their users would always be ready strong to yield to the demand for food supply.

Chapter Twenty-One

The Sharia Law through Gabriel (Jibrīl)

While Jesus was teaching holiness to Jews, they were busy plotting to kill him because, they said, he was doing away with some of the practices they had regarded as laws of their forefathers. One of such laws was the punishment of women for committing adultery [men accomplices were not punished.]

They felt that Jesus made them ashamed when he challenged them to throw stones at the woman who they'd brought to him, accusing her of having committed adultery.

They didn't believe that they were guilty, even though that's how they felt from the beginning when he urged them to throw their stones. Later, they felt not guilty because they believed that a man was entitled to as many wives as he could afford, and as such, a married man going unto another woman was not a crime but, rather, a crime for a married woman who had no right to having many men.

Now, this was and still is one of the ways Satan chose to juxtapose truth with falsehood in the human world. He has changed the meaning of marriage and remained partial towards women. He has maintained that a woman is for every man, so he continues to give men the desire to want every woman they lay their eyes on while keeping the woman home as property for the men to use in any kind of way they like.

The Jews refused to abandon cultures and traditions, so when Jesus had died and returned to Heaven, he sent his archangel Gabriel to Saudi Arabia next door to Israel to give a message to the Jews who were there [in Saudi Arabia] as traders and religious clerics for them to go back to tell their people that God had a message for them.

Unfortunately, they refused to accept a Saudi as a Prophet of God whom they often bragged about as their God alone.

Important among a few things that God wanted to tell the Jews was that they were now allowed to maintain every cultural aspect that had to do with maintaining decency, such as the law of adultery. But his instruction was intended to bring equity before the law. Under the new instruction men of Israel were called on to do as the women were required to do. It meant for both men and women to abstain from adultery, and wherever adultery was found, both the man and the woman who committed the act together were to be punished, and if they agreed that the punishment should be death by stoning or hanging, that was acceptable by God as long as it was meant to bring deterrence and sanity to the community.

God sent them this message because He wanted mankind to keep some of the harsh laws of the gods since they had good intentions to deter or cut down human excesses.

Unfortunately, Mohammad was rejected as a Prophet to the Jews, and as such, his messages were disregarded and excluded from the Bible.

In fact, the Jews sought to kill him as a perfect way to silence him and bring an end to his preaching. So, a great war ensued, but the Lord God abided with Mohammad.

Mohammad was then forced into founding a new religious movement that offered not much from the old Jewish religious book of history and laws. He then adopted the same Jewish tradition of stoning an adulterous person, and they called it "Sharia" as the death penalty for sexual sin.

It was meant for both men and women who committed adultery, but I don't know why women alone are still punished whenever there is a case of adultery in Mohammadism.

In this new era from this book, the Lord has commanded me to tell us all that whoever [man or woman] wants to marry should be ready to stay married, but not double game anymore, and whoever chooses not to marry should declare it so and continue to do so until judgment time.

God believes that it is better to serve one master than to serve two masters at the same time. He also believes that doing one thing at a time helps to simplify the judgment process. That is, if a person is for Him (God), he/she must stay for Him so that the person's shortcomings shall be made simpler to justify than be a double-minded person who shall make justification and the granting of grace difficult in Heaven when judgment comes.

God has seen how people get married but continue to engage in promiscuity. He has seen how people pollute their partners with diseases when the other chooses to be faithful.

Chapter Twenty-Two

Polygamy

The world is moving forward, doing away with certain things that were done in the old, so that we now have two main categories of people in our modern societies; those who are living from the early nineteenth century are labeled as old-school guys, considered to having outdated ideas, while those who were born in the most recent years have labeled themselves as modern guys. But is it true that we have actually done away with certain practices of the old, or we have just turned them the other way around? If you ask me before I can deliver my message from the Spirit World, I'll tell you that we have just turned certain things around, even for the worst, unlike for the better in the old-school days. One such practice is polygamy, or one man having several wives.

The polygamous way had good intentions or purpose in

the old days. Respected and perfectly conducted, it curbed promiscuous practices to the extent that adultery and fornication were taboos that were punishable in the societies. It helped to preserve women to go untouched for God to manifest Himself into a physical being. So, Jesus was born unto a virgin woman.

But see how modern society has turned this same polygamous style to the worst. The people of the modern world say it is wrong for one man to marry many wives, but though they're married, they still have a bunch of different women everywhere they go.

Even the women, too, say they cannot have a mate, but they are still willing to share their boyfriends with their friends.

The worst is happening when they go as two or three or four to take turns with one man in the same room, plus all those ugly things that go on there in that process. Oh, sodomity, oh gomorality, oh seductivity!!!!

So, why did the people practice polygamy? Well, they had several reasons so we will make efforts to deal with them one by one.

(1) *Obedience to God:* Ancient men often died in large numbers in wars, so it brought a scarcity of men. Since women were left over all the time, polygamous practice solved the problem for every woman to get married and keep to her husband so as to avoid the spread of satanic maggots, which in the modern world are called "sexual diseases."

It made women obey God's law to remain faithful

because He is a jealous God who doesn't like to share His food with disobedient/disrespectful/arrogant children of His. This was and is His stance since the day Satan chose his own path.

Unfortunately, the practice of not being married but free to have sex all over the place has exacerbated the process of spreading satanism through sex, and is causing starvation in God's Kingdom.

But one thing that is confirmed to me in full as of the time of this book is that God's Spirit is moving very fast to end this world order since, indeed, He is starving. Thus, He finds it very difficult to get the good people He seeks to obtain nourishment from them. This means that Heavens [God's dwelling place and the spheres in which His good angels live as well] is heavily affected in the wake of the promiscuous lifestyle of this world of ours. Other than this number one thing for God, the following examples are purely human-related.

(2) *Economic:* Wealth in the old was measured by how much cattle and food a man had, so the need for wealth gave importance to marrying several wives. When a man married several wives, his wives helped him with farming work, and thus, he became wealthier in society.

But this was also vice versa for every woman wanted a hardworking man to marry or a woman's family needed to give out their daughter to a hardworking man so that their daughter wouldn't be hungry in her husband's house, and they would also have food to eat from the in-law. So, many women did choose to marry very hard-working men regardless of how many wives they had.

This same desire for more riches [cattle and food] brought in the desire to have many children. So, the more wives a man had, the more children he bore, and they turned out to be his workforce.

Even so, there was this other need for girl children who were destined to be used by parents to obtain riches.

It always started with the early years of the girl child when the fiancé started to work for the family every farming year until she had reached puberty to be given out in marriage to her husband.

Then, when her dowries were paid, often Goat and cow along with other things as is in the Grebo culture, the family acquired riches in this way since the goat and cow were due to reproduce every year.

So, there was always the guarantee that the more women a man had, the more children he was bound to have, and the more workforce he had that brought him wealth in society.

(3) *Home assistance*: So, the aging of a man or his wife brought the need for home assistance. In view of all this, older men often took younger women for wives, who then provided most of the home assistance. Such young wives also bore new children for their older husbands, while the children became younger workforces who continued working their fathers' farmlands.

Therefore, the marriage of young girls to older men in

the old days was more economic and, I must admit, more exploitative.

Emphasis on the scarcity of men due to wars: Now, there were women who lost their husbands; they needed to cater to men as it is required under the universal law of who does what.

In order to avoid promiscuity in societies, it was necessary for a man to take another woman who lost her husband if he desired so, so that her woman's duty to a man would have been fulfilled.

Now, there was this respect and a system that was conducted to take away any charges of adultery and fornication. It goes as saying: if a man had not known the woman before going through a marriage procedure as if the woman was yet a virgin, the law of unfaithfulness to his current wife was never applicable, but if he went unto the woman or any other woman without or before marriage rites, then he was guilty of unfaithfulness and adultery. Likewise, if the widow had not known another man since the death of her husband before marrying another, then she was not guilty of fornication.

However, one thing with polygamy that went wrong was the practice of married men taking younger women or widows who needed to be given out to other younger men or widowers who were not married but ready for marriage. This went against equal distribution.

Difference of old times and new times

Unfortunately, today's marriages are more economic-based rather than a necessity, while yesterday's marriages were necessity-based as polygamy provided an economic solution to men, which gave rise to having large families.

This means that marriage was a compulsory thing to do unlike today's system. And modern polygamy (having girl-friends all around) has got to be an economic drain.

However, today, polygamy could still be necessary IF the world was ready to do the right thing for God. That is, since God's major concern is for mankind to put a stop to promiscuous lifestyles; in order for every man to have a woman or every woman a man, every society could choose to take a census of both males and females so as to begin a process of equal distribution of women to men. This means putting up the names and faces of all unmarried people so that men would begin to make their choices of women.

Surely, the practice of putting up names and faces of people is done right now as Match-Making on the internet, but not enough to meet God's standard. What is happening now needs federal involvement to pass laws that will make the process a legal means of obtaining a wife and a husband and to strengthen the laws of marriage that will issue stronger punishments for breaking marriage laws.

So, when the census results show that there are more women than men, then the process of redistribution (two wives to one man) begins, but if a particular society chooses not to practice polygamy as an unfair distribution of women or men, then an intermarriage system must be employed. Under intermarriage law, a county or country may sign an agreement with another to exchange surpluses. This exchange method may involve bringing in more men from another region that has more men so as to make up for the remaining women who need men or the other way around.

Shockingly, the News of Promiscuous sex in the human world resonates so badly in Heavens, so much so that it is a grave concern to God. It sounds like the news of global warming that science says endangers the future of the human world. We will learn why it is bad news to God elsewhere in this book.

Why were female angels absent among early messengers?

October 26, 2019@11:26 PM, I have just been told that the women of Heaven came to earth along with their male counterparts in those biblical days, but they remained confined to their duties as maintenance spirits of God. They acted like a mechanic engineer who travels on a convoy, doing nothing else throughout the journey unless there is a mechanical fault that requires their expertise. So, their sitting in one place unless there was a need for them to move was the reason why they didn't show up among God's messengers who brought and carried loads [information and powers of healing and all other things] to and from.

I tell you, if your eyes were lucky enough to have seen what the male angels brought to earth or carried back to

Heaven, you must have seen that what the Bible called messages/information were heavy loads that moved through the layers of the Heavens all the time. That's why God gave me an analogy of how invisible powers can be determined.

Chapter Twenty-Three

Payload analogy

Let's imagine what science calls a "Payload." The angel told me to search Google for the meaning of payload, and when I did, I found: (1) A *payload* is an explosive warhead carried by a missile and, (2) In computing and telecommunications, a *payload* is the part of transmitted data that is the actual intended message.

Now, I ask you this question: have you ever seen those messages that travel through wire systems with your naked eyes? Of course not, no one has ever seen voices and images with his/her eyes, but yet computer technology is capable of measuring quantity (Payload) so as to determine how much of it is to be transmitted/sent to a particular destination. In military science, no one has ever seen how much destructive power (Fire Energy) a single missile carries, but yet its damages on a target are beyond human comprehension.

That's how much loads angels, which are spiritual (invisible) forces, carry as messages that we cannot see.

So, when we talk about women's silence in the early days, it originated in the Spirit Realm, where the angelic women were always and are still doing the same today by sitting quietly while taking care of the maintenance aspect of their male counterparts who work very hard to keep Heavens running.

This is the true-life story of women and men in Heavens, but when the angelic women came down to earth [now known as female demons] to redeem human women from the abuse of men of the earth, they started working as men do and that's the beginning of women workers in every field men find themselves in today, which marks the beginning of "Equal Rights & Equal opportunities."

Chapter Twenty-Four

Human's Will-Power

The purpose of reporting these stories is no longer about stopping such practices; rather, it's about telling the truth about how human beings arrived in the present upside-down world. However, anyone who has ears to hear and chooses to set things right for himself/herself is acceptable to the Lord God. All he/she needs do is to make proper use of his/her Will-Power; a very powerful tool from God embedded in all of us to use to be able to accept or reject a command from any force in the air.

These things (different human activities) have long become seeds planted in people all over the world in different styles by these spirits. So, everything that the generation of this millennium sees now is just the fruit of the seeds.

Thus, children are born wayward from long-time seeds planted to produce generations of drunkenness, generations of prostitution, generations of promiscuity/cheats, generations of warriors, generations of liars, gossipers, stealers, killers, cunningness, witch crafting, sorcery, and magicians (church prophets and prophetesses.)

This practice of planting Spiritual seeds in humans can be compared to what is happening in technological countries where they create video games that require the use of weapons and shooting to kill, horror movies, pornographies, and other nurturing images that are used to grow young children into lives of wickedness. This means that teaching kids how to shoot and kill is a form of nurturing young minds towards the pleasure of taking lives as opposed to seeing life as a vital thing to protect. This explains the meanings of the other activities mentioned above.

Even now, the science community is becoming more diverse as children have started creating little inventions in tech-oriented communities. But the seeds in every man are not greater than his/her Willpower; it remains a matter of choosing between two things, like when you have two communication towers or radio stations, and you must decide on which one to make your favorite station.

Condoms

The purpose of planting these spiritual seeds has been behind the collection of semen long ago by the marine world. Earlier, I said they're against men's progress, and now I say they target only men to store up resources that they can use on themselves without touching their fellow women. So, they introduced the condom system to collect the sperm/semen of men that would be used for **cloning** (duplication) when they perform their erestospasses on them ("**Erestospasses**" is a spiritual mix of a male's stamen and female's estrogen.)

Now, let me (PAUL) make clear to every reader of this book that strange words like "Erestospasses" plus familiar words like "Stamen" and "Estrogen," were just forced down my tongue by the Spirit on November 1, 2018 at 2:54 P.M. while I was drafting the manuscript of this book. As I was typing, the Spirit came down on me and forced me to write each word before allowing me to check each one up on my computer that afternoon. The Spirit dictated the spelling of these words to me, and this became the case with all other strange words and familiar ones anyone may find in all of my books. So, whatever the dictionary's meanings are, they don't apply to this book.

Chapter Twenty-Five

Do female spirits get pregnant?

Erestospasses is the heavenly (Spiritual) means by which angels are made in Heaven so that there is no impregnation of female angels since sex there doesn't mean the same as it does on earth.

Medical science has already arrived at that. All that is required is to collect the two fluids from any healthy sources and combine them synthetically (IVF), and then babies are produced.

But the Spirit revealed that there is a risk to that. The Spirit said the kinds of humans to be produced may run the risk of being unable to reproduce other humans, which would subject humanity to synthetic beings that would slow the human population's growth.

I was told the sort of people to be created would be subjected to "Infralight (a very piercing light)," which would cause infertility because it blindfolds certain cells in the body of such human creatures. A few may be lucky, though.

The Tendering system

These draconian women are infatuated (crazy) with tendering men unto one another as goods because they don't see these men as possessions as it is under marriage. This is what happens when women give men to each other as passes and vice versa.

Oh my God, they are crazy. They don't go for a damn. They control sensuality (the ability to be attracted to beauty in all its forms, attracted to worldly pleasure that includes singing & dancing, all that goes along with drinking, smoking, and sexing to the highest order.) This now makes this world Sodom and Gomorrah: The End Time society in which sex played a significant role in its destruction. The last Doom is at hand.

So, on this day, March 5, 2019 @9:10, A.M., here in Sacramento, California, USA, the Spirit of the Lord Jesus came to me to give me this extraordinary message. He said all these things [Singing and dancing, drinking and smoking, and taking women to bed] that we're talking about are in no way wrong to do, for God had created all things for specific purposes.

They're good, but the fact that Satan has stepped in to create greed (excessive use or need) for these things in mankind because he (Satan) knows the power in them (the things), so the evil [not the good] in them has been achieved to the most considerable extent.

He preached to me this morning [like a man sobbing] to tell me that Satan is very much aware of the power that is in the minerals used in making weapons and weapons of mass destruction. That's why he (Satan) is taking advantage of them to cause strong desires by nations [including Israel, the supposed land of peace education through the Bible] around the world to make military adventures a high priority that is slowly heading the world towards destruction by human hands.

He tells me, saying, tell my people that we (Almighty God and I) are frustrated with the world and are wrapping up quickly to end everything very soon. He says not even denuclearization of North Korea or Iran shall bring peace into the world while other nations like Saudi Arabia and others are warming up for the thing that other countries are fighting to increase or advance more as others are told not to have.

The appetite for self-defense is increasing by the day because other First Nations didn't choose the course of peace by avoiding aggressions and armament, so there is no way to create peace by disarming others with the power of advanced weapons pointed at their doorsteps. That's the Voice of the Spirit of the Lord this morning.

Chapter Twenty-Six

AIDS, Condom, and Dildo

Don't forget when I told you in the beginning about the coming down of Mobee Salabatees, the first woman, who came from Heaven and came unto Satan. I said she consulted with God that she wanted to set physical women free from the brutal hands of physical men who operated under the influence of Satan and his men. I also said God permitted her, but in God's discretion, it was to strike at Satan and to create a balance between female spirits and male spirits. Still, God chose to leave whatever came out of Mobee's operation to the end when He [God] would have to judge all who did what they did in the world.

In the same vein, I said that though the women came down with good intentions, unlike the men, they changed into wicked forces when they began to feel the bodies of physical men. This change in attitudes brought about division among them, so there are moderate and draconian women forces today.

Therefore, the topic above that I'm about to discuss has no official approval from God, no matter how they favor God's own choice of life. Yet He will gladly acquit those who choose to do the right thing to the end, while He shall convict those who choose to be wicked in reprisal to the end.

What this means is that the way each spirit uses God's power determines which side that spirit belongs to, and this brings even the pagans and atheists to redemption during judgment day.

This means that anything that we call "disease" in our world today is also God's power used negatively, like a doctor administering an overdose of the same medicine that heals. [What is "disease" in our world is different in the Spirit World, where it is called "Diyohseseur," meaning, "Let's break up or disintegrate or disassemble"].

The way pagans and atheists shall come to redemption is that in our world from yesterday to today, some who go to church every day are secretly doing wicked things more than some who don't at all so that when God brings down His Grace (grading system), many will be shocked to see some Christians falling short of God's glory. In contrast, some pagans may pass through the narrow gate.

Christians should stop boasting that accepting Jesus as Lord and Savior is enough to send them to Heaven. If that were so, then Jesus wouldn't have required Christians to do the right things. If that were so, there wouldn't be judgment waiting for them to separate the good from the bad among them. The judgment of pagans and atheists can be seen in the EXTRAS section of this book.

This scenario also explains why churches need not argue about what God thinks of healing powers in the churches, even as they run very parallel to satanic powers. It all depends on the intent of the administrator; is he/she using it for God's purpose or his/her own purpose?

Here, of course, it gets difficult to determine how it becomes for God's purpose or personal purpose, but one easy way to determine that is how to compare freeing Satan's victims from spiritual entanglements to how your desire for gains for the work affects your decisions. That is, you have the power to heal, but you put a price tag on it, and that turns your work into pure business like the pagans, far beyond what the Bible would require of you. Or do you turn the same power of God around to cause harm to the people? Doing so would amount to a doctor misusing his/her professional duties to inflict damage on patients since the same power that heals has a way of harming as well, depending on how it's applied.

Since I'm just a storyteller but not a biblical writer, I've tried to avoid using Bible quotations everywhere because I leave all that to those who teach the Bible. So, I want to remind you that the Christian book of the Bible makes it clear that God was the one who gave power to Satan and that all powers belong to God. This means that there is no single knowledge that Satan possesses that God doesn't have, except that Satan is in the habit of misusing every power of God to his personal advantage [remember the suicide bombers who may use a personal vehicle for evil, thus changing the intended purpose for the vehicle to evil personal satisfaction].

I also remember watching a video screen that told the story of Moses's encounter with Pharaoh in Egypt. In that story, God empowered Moses's staff into a serpent that swallowed all the staff serpents of Pharaoh's magicians.

The point I'm making here is that God is the master, in fact, the owner, of all the powers that Satan has, so theologians must stop thinking that God doesn't know anything about what man calls evil, like diseases we're about to discuss and yes, they're right on the other hand since God doesn't use His powers to hurt us, but Satan does, and that's why it is just good to say that God doesn't make diseases.

That's why I keep saying throughout my books that God has come to us again to explain Himself. He knows all the confusions we're having, the accusations we have been laying against Him, and how we have turned His word into our own benefits.

For example, we've turned the Bible into a weapon to kill when we use it to pray to God on the battlefields. We've turned the Bible into business when we use it in the mortuary to pray for more dead bodies to work on as a boom to our business. We've turned the Bible into a play toy when we use it every evening to go on missions that God has already condemned; the robbers pray every evening before setting out, the harlots pray every night before going out, and all those people pray with the Bible while they say-God says we should confess our sins, and He will forgive us.

He told me to tell everyone that He is not and has not been the responder to those prayers, but the one in the lower heaven has been. To explain, He gave me the Information Superhighway or Communication cycle.

Therefore, the activities of the two women's kingdoms discussed herein reflect their own choices of behavior.

So, I've been permitted to say sexual diseases are counter-attacks from the moderate women who think by inflicting these conditions on humanity; there will be a little calm and peace between God and humanity. They think that many people will be scared away from promiscuous sex and will choose marriage and commitment. Still, on the other hand, the battle continues with the introduction of condoms by the draconian women. The worst attack is the bloody attack on humanity, and it seems to define the objective of Christianity (obey the Lord's commandment or else there is a doom awaiting you.)

So, with diseases and untimely deaths all over the place, I think [my opinion] the doom of suffering begins right here on earth even before judgment comes, so those of us stubborn enough to yield to the fleshly things of this world shall continue to suffer diseases and early deaths before our appointed time.

AIDS virus is a bloody attack that is consuming the peace of relationships, but the draconian group tends to provide solutions for victims through retrovirus drugs and condoms.

Other contributing factors help the AIDS virus to perforate the core of the central system of its victims, and as such, these victims fit into a particular category that is not right now for disclosure for psychological reasons. [*This matter shall be suitable for disclosure during our lecture time and is important for the purpose of how to correct (erase) your wrongs while you're still alive so that when judgment comes, you shall have a better score in the Lord's Book of records:*

> *"He who overcomes will thus be clothed in white garments, and I will not erase his name from the book of life, and I will confess his name before My Father and before His angels" (Rev. 3:5). "Nothing unclean, and no one who practices abomination and lying, shall ever come into it, but only those whose names are written in the Lamb's book of life"*
>
> *— (Rev. 21:27)*

Yet the Draconian women have set out again to help the gang of women who men have abused and, therefore, reject the touches of men by choosing to have sex without needing men. Such abused women have been benefiting from another sexual tool (dildo) made by the draconian women to help them flux their bodies (Cleanse the body of unwanted properties.)

Dildo is also applicable to other women and men for peculiar reasons.

The question now is: Can we ever find peace in the hands of these forces? The answer has always been NO. Not even science can give us peace, except the word of God, which tells us what to do to avoid all the problems we're facing.

Chapter Twenty-Seven

It's their war game

Whether traditional or scientific, the cycle of Diseases and Healing is a war game constantly played by warring factions of the air.

What distinguishes one particular tribe from another is the cultural and traditional practices of those who make up the tribe. These differences begin with the terminologies they use as their language and the things they believe in as their way of life, such as what makes a taboo (a forbidden thing) and what herbs, food types, and skills they have that are different from those of another group of people.

All these things that define a group of people into a tribe have been introduced to them for ages by a particular god or goddess (a force in the air that hangs over them). That is why one tribe uses certain plants to inflict, repel, and heal a particular attack or disease, while, in most cases, different plants or a part of the same plant are used in other areas for the same purpose.

The way we see these boundaries between our communities, that's how the air space has been divided and bordered among the forces, too, and the same way we see quarrels, wars, and healing solutions in our communities, that's how the forces that control us, do. I mean, they are the ones who fight among themselves over territorial control.

Every time one god or goddess sends an attack that inflicts injuries, the other to whom the attack has been directed wherein its human benefactors get injured, tells the human population it controls what plant to use for the repel or repair of that situation and that's how we have all the different diseases and healing solutions with traditional herbs and scientific medicines in our world today. Therefore, whatever harm befalls each of us on earth with its alternate solution, whatever way, is a war game played by the forces of the air.

Therefore, we're their battlegrounds and the victims. When we yield to their callings, and we fall dead, they flee out of our bodies like a bird leaving a falling branch of a tree on which it perched every morning, afternoon, and evening; yes, they just go away.

Right now, God is telling you that you still have a chance to change your ways before the end comes. Do not doubt anything, no matter how you look at this book. This is a sincere voice from the Lord as He calls on you to change.

Question of a word for men who have women for pay

I have a case study: In the sex trade, there are two participants; one is the seller, and the other is the buyer. But why are women alone labeled as Prostitutes and the bad ones?

Here's the answer: The answer is rooted in who initiated the whole idea of giving sex to get something to live on. And, of course, the woman did.

So go back and review the story about Mobee's first journey from Heaven to Satan in the Spirit realm, then review the story about the goddess Ishtar of ancient Mesopotamia here on earth.

New word for men who pay women for sex

Yet, I think it is about time now to adopt a new word for men who intentionally offer money to some women to entice them into sex despite the woman's marriage status. So, I think men are "prostitutes," herein referred to as "postactors" (post actors). This means women started it, but men do the same now, and it goes like this: the man tells the woman-I like you, woman, and I'll help you in any way if you accept, even for a fling. Most men say this to women even when the women don't beg them or request them for money. In this case, then, the man is the initiator of sex for pay and should be guilty of the crime of prostitution, while the woman is also guilty of postaction [post action].

Chapter Twenty-Eight

The government system

At the close of the preface, I recognized how theologians may think when they come to this portion in particular. They may feel that I've deviated from Spirituality to the politics of the earth. Still, no, that's not the case, just that the spirit of God [the angel of God] that schooled me on this matter of the government system of the earth says these systems are the way the gods/forces of the earth have chosen to use each part of God to do their works in the world. So, they repurposed them to suit their desires for how they wanted to rule the earth.

Yet I wouldn't be surprised at all if any theologian thinks that I'm speculating, and that is because they've become used to the things they know and have taught over the centuries.

Another reason I wouldn't blame them is because such thinking is meant to bring out what happened to Moses's contemporary men when they confused depictions in the heavenly garden with the physical geography of their time so that they thought Moses was talking about the physical earth. Still, later in the book of Ezekiel (Ezk. 28:13-17), God showed them where Moses's Garden of Eden could be located. Yet, they stuck their minds to what they imagined so that the actual information God passed on to mankind received corruptible teaching among the children of God up to today.

That's why I want you [my reader] to realize that God has allowed these things to be discussed among us right now, just when the world is experiencing the conflicts these good ideas of God are causing. See the EXTRAS section of this book.

Before going further, I assume you may have read all the pieces that give us (every human being) proof that we're just duplicates/photocopies of all that Heavens (the invisible world) is. For this reason, I'm set again to report to you how the earth has received a governing system, the practice of God making rules & regulations from Heaven, and how the earth has adopted different forms of government to emulate the different parts of God, not necessarily His governing system.

So, what is considered a part of God? A part of God is all that constitutes Him, including all His gifts that do not change or distinguish good from evil. That's why His Democracy (God's granting of Will-Power to all) is one part of Him. But any decision He makes is subject to change due to circumstances like giving of life (the right given to angels to give life), which is a law because He can choose to change His mind and take away life based on certain conditions.

That's how death (a right given to angels to bring back Souls) comes in, and even death He can choose to postpone.

Originally, the Heavens were like this one big United States of America that has its own subdivisions, which the American people call States. The States in the Heavens are its spheres (All the different types of layers of the Air/Atmosphere).

Everything was just one, meaning that Heavens (All the spheres) had only one leader [King, otherwise called President on earth], who happened to be God, the creator Himself.

God's Throne (Upper Heaven) was precisely like Washington D.C., which has legal control over all the States in the United States. All states, though they may have their local laws, are subject to the Federal government. This made Heaven a peaceful place, like the U.S.A., to live in until one of its kind, Lucifer, rebelled [refused] to follow the laws.

So, a war broke out [the war was a scuffle between Lucifer and the arresters], but they were unable to overpower him until he escaped out of that Heaven [the primary sphere in which God Himself dwells; the spirits call it His Throne/Chair because He hardly moved like one giant equipment that stationed at one spot to work but it's most preferred to the word "Capital"] down to another sphere [the spirits call it the "Earth" but it's the mass of air that hangs directly over the earth crust] in which the forces reside to operate the earth crust.

Lucifer's escape from God's presence [most often referred to as "Heaven"] shook the place, for nearly all popularly adored him. Heavens turned feverish for some time, for He was an important part of God.

The scene is similar to when any vital machinery gets damaged in a factory; the factory goes without work for some time. All this happened because He didn't leave alone but with other important people who empathized with him.

This was the beginning of division in the Heavens, and the Heavens experienced two governing systems: God Himself headed one in the lesser part, while Satan headed the other in the larger part. [The area God controls is smaller than that of Satan's control since a smaller area of Heaven was considered to be developed yet.] This is the same as what the earth was destined to inherit. On earth, the number of humans Satan dominates is larger than the number of faithful Christians he dominates.

This time, let me escape what happened in the Spirit realm when God drove away Lucifer, now Satan, and man, and let me come straight down to the ground where we now have governments on our own.

When mankind evolved out of the ground and became a full-grown creature, he started to make his own rules and regulations, which he called "Laws," to guide him and his family in how to do things.

In the structure, the head of the family (often a man) became the chief custodian (maker and enforcer) of the family laws. Then, the system expanded to a trim community level, where elders of a few families came together to make their own laws to guide them in dealing with one another. The Provincial law system followed, and eventually, the country law system came about to bring together a larger group of people under one leadership. At the country level, mankind finally arrived at what Heaven looked like.

But when the human world began to adopt its own governing system, it developed many different forms of government, starting with Kingship (lifetime service) and tenures (short-term service).

Kingship became how the gods of our lands (the Forces in the air that put words on every man's tongue) interpreted who God is in Heaven. And under Kingship, the gods also expressed to mankind certain attributes of God as He has done towards angels in Heaven.

So the Lord, our God, has come to explain how the world has received so many types of rulers in different parts and how all these forms have been compressed under only two major forms of governments competing for control of the world now.

Therefore, **Kingship** is God making Himself the ruler over everything forever. This behavior of God [Could] be one of the reasons why Satan, being Lucifer, envied his creator and decided to be like Him. And that's why he (Satan) made himself King after falling to the Earth to rule on his own.

In expressing Kingship [For God it is done with love], the King, having been vested with the power of making final decisions with or without others, often goes tough on certain things aimed at curbing down the excesses of subjects and when this happens several other words emerge like Totalitarianism, Dictatorship & Absolutism; all words have been exact but little bit differ in strengths. For example, *Totalitarianism* may be a ruler's frequent way of insisting on whatever he believes is necessary to do without causing bodily harm to people. At the same time, Dictatorship may be the same behavior and attitude towards issues. Still, it comes with the force of brutality on the people whenever they bent on objecting, and then comes Absolutism, which seems to have the permission of the ruler's Councilmen.

Absolutism on earth may be a bunch of corrupt leaders who put enough power in the hands of the ruler to make final judgments whenever and however he pleases. Such leaders or Councilmen may choose to bow to whatever oppression comes from their dictator on their citizens as long as he makes them his favorite with whom he plunders the nation's wealth.

These different ways of expressing Kingship continued until some nations experienced a takeover by a small group of wealthy people who chose to have everything to themselves to the greatest extent. This brought another word: "Oligarchy." So, **Oligarchism** may embody all three expressions above except that it is of a small group of wealthy people.

The main reason that God decided to reveal the government system by the gods of our lands is to talk about Communism/Socialism and Democracy/capitalism that we have competing now in the last days. What do they mean?

Communism and Socialism are interrelated but differ in a little way, so let me take them one by one:

Communism

Communism- is an act of a group of people communing (coming together) to work together or combine efforts for the benefit of all. It is a part of God. It defines Heavens. That means all works done in Heavens are done on a communal level. All Heavenly dwellers work together and share everything because no one owns anything there except God, who freely gives everything to all angels.

Communism [a system without ownership], therefore, makes Heavens peaceful and free of envy/jealousy, corruption, and backbiting.

The first time Lucifer expressed envy/jealousy over God, the idea of doing things by oneself [ownership] tended to be very favorable, but his act caused him to fall out of God's presence.

So, several other angels (firstly males and secondly females) chose to fall out and live and do things on their own. Still, close to the time God decided to discuss this topic with the human world, people (the forces) of the Heavens began to realize that pure Communism under the Almighty God is good. They have seen and gotten tired of fighting and quarreling among themselves. They continue to retrospect each passing day how peaceful they lived in Heaven before they fell to the ground.

Socialism

Socialism- is love and friendship. By being social [being together or being friends], people accept and appreciate one another, and when they appreciate one another, they are happy to work together and share meals. That's why the two words are inseparable. They're the true meaning of what God wants His community (places and their peoples) to be, and that's what Heavens is.

Since we're now discussing sins out of Satan's way of turning God's system of governing around, let's take a brief look at what sin is.

How did the word "Sin" come about?

The word 'Sin,' evolved out of God's way of saying "Satan's Intent" or "Satan's Intent never to return."

All those who live in Heaven are in peace, and any time one experiences jealousy or any form of deviation from the right way, that person is automatically thrown out of Heaven and sent straight to Earth like a shooting star. It is an automated computer setting in Heaven; it just happens, and no one has to report it to God before He acts anymore.

Did the Bible say anything about putting someone out of the church for sin? Yes, the Bible said so, but with caution and guidance:

"It is actually reported that there is sexual immorality among you, and of a kind that is not tolerated even among pagans, for a man has his father's wife. And you are arrogant! Ought you not rather to mourn? Let him who has done this be removed from among you. For though absent in body, I am present in spirit; and as if present, I have already pronounced judgment on the one who did such a thing. When you are assembled in the name of the Lord Jesus, and my spirit is present, with the power of our Lord

Jesus, you are to deliver this man to Satan for the destruction of the flesh, so that his spirit may be saved in the day of the Lord"

— (1 Cor. 5:1-13 ESV).

"If he refuses to listen to them, tell it to the church. And if he refuses to listen even to the church, let him be to you as a gentile and a tax collector"

— (Matt. 18:17 ESV).

So you see, since the world was still in its primitive (embryonic) stage, Jesus had to give the responsibility to the investigative team of church people. Still, I tell you this: the world is advancing fast towards the heavenly way of detecting wrongdoers when we hear of facial technology in which period everyone shall be monitored, and the technology to arrest is yet to come to grab law breakers immediately, among others for whatever crime it's designed for to arrest.

That's how Heaven is automated, and that's how Heaven is sophisticated. However, these sciences of Heaven shall receive corruptible uses on earth, and that's why God still needs to destroy the world despite its sophistication so that He shall replace them with the same but incorruptible ones.

What did Jesus's lifestyle teach about government?

Communism/Socialism [take them as one] is the lifestyle that Jesus brought to earth and introduced to his followers by asking everyone to sell his property to follow him [that embodied - get all that you own so that we all could own and share them.]

By introducing this, bringing everything to the Lord or to the Church while sharing bread on the same table with them all, he had hoped that the disciples would have continued living like this or even improved it better by farming together to have food for themselves after his mission had ended on earth.

Jesus' ultimate aim was to make Christians a communal group of people on earth who would have done away with the practices of the pagans who delight in the things of the world for their satisfaction. The pagans devote all their time to chasing after material gathering through trade [skills] and commerce [marketing things.]

Where did the world go wrong?

If the disciples had continued in this line of living, each country could have had a Christian community right now [described as "Mission Town"] running on the other side, different from a secular community [loose life] that is bound by government dictates.

Analogy of Spiritual Responses	Communication Cycle
Communication starts from what the heart desires and sends to the brain [mind], and the mind sends it into the air [Spiritual world] from where various spirits act on human desires. Just as special creatures gather for any particular thing, like man wastes sugar and sugar ants come to feed, or when a man drops poop, and flies gather to feed, so do different spirits come to different physical materials and physical activities.	

Secular town	**Mission town**
*In this town; sensual spirits [all spirits of worldliness] come to earth to feed on physical materials like drinks and narcotics, to help man sing and dance to the songs of danmines [songs made by singing demons]. *In this town; everything is violent: Sex is brutal, songs and dances are brutal, sex is	*In this town; loving spirits [angels] come to earth to feed on physical materials like communion items [all the things the heart has chosen for God's spirits to manifest in], to help man sing and dance gospels of nonmines [songs made by singing angels]. *In this town; everything is calm: Sex is gentle, songs and

| mismatched and full of fantasy, eating and drinking are overdone. | dances are soft and soul soothing, sex is matched [matchmaking in today's world is a copy but half of the process], eating and drinking are sequential [bit-by-bit]. | |

Secular and Mission Towns mixed up

Music: Explosive and violent sounds penetrate all layers more than the Heavens can withhold, just as violent prayers strike Satan so much like gun bullets, even though this violence originates from the repented spirits of the lower order.

Government: Christians in government hardly fulfill their Christian duties as they make laws to satisfy both secular activities and Christian lives.

Work environment: Christians in workplaces are bound by the laws of their masters, and as such, they often go against their own faith in obedience to work ethics. Sometimes corrupt bosses coerce [by threats] subordinates to ungodly work practices.

Church worshipers: Church worshippers [most often] go to church on Sunday mornings to sing and dance with nonmines [singing angels], then they go to secular parties or nightclubs in the evening to sing and dance with danmines [singing demons].

> **Sex:** All the things [styles & activities] unbelievers do are done by believers as well. In fact, after God had clothed the man [covered their nakedness in the Garden], man has decided to be naked outside the Garden so you can see nakedness in all places around the world.
>
> **The two masters:** Mankind has so much delight in serving the two masters [God and Satan], but God shall judge based on man's best heart desire [how hard did each of us try to do the things that please God against the things that didn't please Him {this may be put as- all good deeds against all evil deeds + God's Grace}].
>
> **Money rules:** Couples do not [much] curdle each other anymore for heat, but the quill/blanket does for each person while the other is out there for several days to work for money.

The evitable is inevitable

What Jesus was trying to establish for Christians has defined the period in which mankind lives now [the same time this book has come to tell the story behind the story]. In this period of technology, Christians would have had the technological skills to use for their well-being without wasting their good time chasing after money before getting anything for themselves. Christians could have been excused from all corrupt practices because they would have had no reasons to be corrupt. Christians could have been like those living in the Heavens, where peace exists, while the pagans would have been the ones living in Akkuepus/Aquebus (Satan's city/Enclave), where greed, self-style, and brutality exist.

Unfortunately, those who are called the disciples of Jesus [Jesus' followers after he left them] have returned to their old ways; their old ways include the time when Peter spent most of his time looking for fish in the rivers and others who were involved in government works, as well as the various means by which the pagans gathered the riches of the world for themselves.

Impure Communism

The emergence of Communism/Socialism [I learned] has its roots in Russia, a vast Asian country. The current President of that Country is "Vladimir Putin," he is labeled as one of the world's most challenging leaders at the time of this book [this is 2018].

As is the case with everything that falls outside God's standard, Communism in the world has been. It is a perfect system in Heaven that is worth living, but it has lost its validity [the very essence of having it] to the world's people because ownership [this is mine] has been introduced with it.

Those whom the spirits helped to introduce it to that part of the world had been told the importance of it, but they were also told to own properties for themselves while providing for the general public. They owned things above others and had provisional stores set aside for themselves while they acted like lords over everybody. They taught the people not to worry about anything because they [the people often referred to as peasants] could walk into a particular store and grab things they needed for food. Still, their duty was to work and freely receive whatever they needed.

So you see, the mistake had been made by allowing a specific group of people to own things on their own while others were not allowed. Injustice was done to the masses who looked up to others every morning to see them shining better than they were. The real purpose was thwarted just to force obedience from the masses and to exercise absolute control over the masses so that fighting would set in and killing would follow to ensure the blood supply to the Spirit world.

This is exactly what is happening in communist countries where fighting for wealth has plunged the inhabitants into various wars in families, organizations, and societies. Killing is the language of everyday's news.

Now, we have entered the robotic age in science. We're supposed to use more robots to do our work, just as the Spiritual world uses us [human beings] as their robots to do more of what is required on earth to keep the Heavens running. Communist societies are better positioned to use robots to do their work since it will be easier to adopt the culture of people working fewer hours on a rotational basis to get better pay for assisting robots with minor jobs.

The fact that all Spiritual Forces are trained in every field of work in their world makes it easier for them to change shifts by seconds in a continuous chain, so we feel this process of one spirit coming to work while another leaves as a breathing system on our bodies. This is how mankind is supposed to exchange shifts on a second-by-second basis with good pay in the near robotic world.

Democracy

Democracy- is another good part of God in Heaven. It is God's way of letting people be half-independent. By being half independent, everyone has the right [permission] to choose for himself/herself. This Right of Permission is a Law or Decree in Heaven. In fact, God decreed for Himself not to tamper with this right of every man and woman.

Under this right, everyone goes to the food center [on earth, it is called "Buffet"], and he/she chooses anything to eat without paying money. In the food center, there is a variety of food prepared and set everywhere where people go to pick any food type of their choice. Oh, I like this!!!

Under this right of choice, Lucifer chose to go on his own to do things for himself, and others followed through. It was under this same decree that God was unable to undo Lucifer, and the Christian book refers to it as "God didn't take power from Satan."

Let's take a break and give you my (PAUL's) story:

Before I became what I am today [a man who hears the voice of the Spirit], I used to argue the Bible. One of my arguments was that God did permit Satan to do what he (Satan) is doing in the world. My use of the word *permission* was meant to say that God actually approved of Satan, and I told Satan is working for God to do what he's doing today.

My purpose in saying this was that the Bible says God has all the power to do anything, including destroying Satan. So, I meant to say that in as much as God didn't destroy Satan, then He (God) agreed to use him as His agent. Many pastors tried to make me understand the meaning of 'permission' according to God's standards, but I didn't understand it until now.

So, all of what I say and write today is not from the teaching of any pastor or theological lecturer but from the direct power of the Spirit Himself. He has commanded me to break down every word of the Bible to the simplest means for the understanding of the little boy/girl in the street without requiring seminary study.

By the definition of democracy in the Heavens, God [being the whole system] should be seen as an automatic machine that is set to run until the time runs out before it stops.

Maybe you haven't gotten me well, so let's go the other

way; you have a cooking machine [Microwave] in your house, it has numbers on it to time it, say for 10 minutes to cook your meal, so you set it on one and zero, and that's number ten (10) then you push the START button and leave to go anywhere you want to go. You wait until ten minutes is complete and then grab your food. What happened right there is that the cooker/microwave stopped automatically right after the ten minutes given to it, which also makes it the right time for the food to get done.

If you look at Satan and everything that is happening today, like the electric cooker set in motion with time to stop, then the whole idea about the end of this world will be avail to you understandably, other than that, sorry for you.

So, democracy is that part of God that got us to this point today. His (God's) own desire not to interfere with everyone's Willpower did stop Him from destroying Satan as soon as he (Satan) rebelled/deviated.

Can you now see how democratic societies are beginning to suffer under their own laws? The right to freedom to do anything you like is getting at the very people who set up the system so much that when anyone does something wrong, he/she begins to invoke the laws governing his/her rights. In fact, under this freedom to do anything you like, sinful acts [the very acts that Christians read about each day in the Bible that constituted the destruction of the old world] are now permitted under democratic principles [don't tamper with anyone's choice of life].

Impure Democracy

Just as communism emerged on the other side of the world, so did European democracy. Its exact place could be attributed to Athens, a city in Attica, Greece. It is located at 37.98 latitude and 23.72 longitude. [In modern geographical settings] Greece is at the crossroads of Europe, Asia, and Africa. Situated on the southern tip of the Balkan Peninsula, it shares land borders with Albania to the northwest, the Republic of Macedonia and Bulgaria to the north, and Turkey to the northeast.

Located on the continent of Europe, Greece covers 130,647.00 square kilometers and has a population of 10,767,827 (updated October 2, 2015, by World Atlas).

The current President of Greece is called "Prokopis Pavlopoulos."

Just as Communism is, so is Democracy in the world. It is a perfect system in Heaven that is worth living, but it lost its validity [the very essence of having it] to the people of the world because ownership [the idea of this is for me] has also been introduced with it. And just as God's democracy [the right He granted to His angels as self-will] was abused in Heavens, so has democracy on earth been abused by those who have it.

What would a free world be like?

Believe me, if the world combines Communism and Democracy, the solution for joblessness and government taking care of everybody in a robotic world looming around is easy to achieve.

I tell you the truth: if the world yields to China's call for BRI as I hear them discussing the importance of Socialism in this link, Why is there a growing global interest in socialism? | Talk with socialists from the UK, Ghana & Lebanon, the world would eventually get better.

> This kind of freedom [democracy] and cooperation [communalism] that exist in Heaven is what God wants on earth. That's why Jesus told His disciples to pray daily so that what is done in Heaven shall be done on earth [this is the basis of the Lord's Prayer].
>
> The Lord's Prayer was Jesus's way of telling His disciples that this age [this period until the rapture comes] is for Satan, which also means that whatever happens in this same period is for Satan. Still, after His (Satan's) period comes the system [Jesus's time to rule] that will be like unto Heaven, and in that new world shall be one system that will combine democracy and communism together wherein there will be no division and no fighting, but peace shall prevail throughout the world.

Why our world is like this?

The whole thing called sin came upon mankind through the same person who invented the sense of 'the right thing to do for yourself,' and he is Satan. He has peacefully lived in democracy since its birth in Athens because he knew from the onset that many people would like to be free and do anything they want. People like to be free from embarrassment by another [exalting above another].

It has worked perfectly for many countries where the right to choose and do anything is preached and taught in schools.

But you see, just as I told you in Heavens, the angels have now started to realize true Communism is a perfect way to go, and so democracy in the world has started to realize its excesses. In democratic societies, rights have exceeded their limits and have begun to be abused by those who should protect them.

The people are corrupt even though they don't want anyone to say it to them. The women are abused even though they accept to be used. The Country has accepted those very things that constitute everything that forced God to end the first world, and the people enjoy it because it is their right to choose whatever they want.

The Church has also joined the world by accepting the very things that it teaches to have constituted the destruction of the old world just because there is a "human right" in these democratic countries.

Now, the two great government systems are competing over the control of the world. Satan is significantly energized, and he is pouring out the weapons of destruction everywhere to be planted in every corner of the earth.

Because ownership has engulfed the minds of the world's people, those who have been ahead don't want to allow another to come to be like them or surpass them. The result now is fear in everybody [new people are fearful of suppression while old people fear leadership defeat], and they're building weapons against each other to support their egos.

The order of the day has now become, I must have this, I must be the head, I must maintain this, and I ALONE must tell them what to do.

I, I & I is the ugliest side of the ownership system in the world of mankind, and [of course] it is dragging everyone towards catastrophe. Whether sooner or later, the fact remains that the world is not safe anymore due to pride.

Chapter Twenty-Nine

EXTRAS

Although many theologians usually downplay the truth about how the Bible didn't say everything mankind needs to know about God, and they refuse to acknowledge publicly that the Bible contains human errors [not God's errors], the theocratic ministry of the Lord Jesus Christ, brought to earth by God in December 2005, is charged with the responsibility to unveil these truths. This section of this book contains a few of them as extras, among other things. Since all these things cannot be written at once, the ministry would be publishing them in tracts from time to time.

Man's Spiritual existence. (What does Latter Days Saints church say?)

In their book, they have a topic, "*Where did I come from?*" written on page 2 of a Bible teaching Tract titled "The Plan of Salvation." In there, they write,

"Your life didn't begin at birth, nor will it end at death. You are made up of a spirit body (sometimes called the soul) and a physical body. Your Heavenly

Father created your spirit, and you lived with Him as a spirit before you were born on earth. You knew and loved Him, and He knew and loved you. This period is called pre-earth life."

Obviously, I have not seen any church that has taught this kind of teaching, as does the Latter Days Saints. It comes close to what the Spirit of God revealed in my school years about man's spiritual existence in the Heavens before becoming physical.

I take this report significant today because it lays the premise of what has been fully disclosed to all the peoples of the earth [through me {an interpreter, a storyteller, and a revelator}] at the end of all the work they [all who reported from the Spirit world] have been doing even before God came to earth the first time in Ur.

Therefore, God told me in 2008 that all the things that I was taught [in the school of the Spirit of God] from 2006 to mid-2008 have been written about by the people who came before me, but their works contained some lapses (gaps) that He [God] has come to correct and fill in during this review period.

Therefore, on the things of man's Spiritual existence, God brought forth to me Ezekiel 28:13-17 to begin the history of Satan's existence in the Garden of Eden where he did wrong things [Satan assumed God's authority and deceived man] before he was thrown down to the Earth.

So, the spirits of God started giving me the details on this Spiritual man, starting with Lucifer [now Satan] in the Garden of Eden and his interaction with man there.

They [the many spirits that came down on earth to me one after another as lecturers on various issues] said to me that everything about today's mission [to review or to go all over the Bible again] hangs entirely on man's ability to get the complete understanding of Spiritual man who was briefly discussed by the prophets to whom the Latter Days Saints bear witness.

Because we now live in the world of technology, I tell you this truth: every new information you may find in this book and all of my books is nothing but the truth that mankind needs before this world will ever pass away. For this reason, He gave me so many analogies to help us understand the things that are Spiritual in the Bible, but mankind has taken to be physical. This book, therefore, is a News Report from the Space world.

However, in discussing all these, I want to remind all Christians that God has come back to earth [now writing through me] to make something very clear in the Bible, which is in Ezk. 28:13-17, focus 13 & 17. In 13, God told us where Satan was (the garden) until He (Lucifer) rebelled/sinned, and in 17, He (God) told us where (to the earth) He sent Lucifer (now Satan). This means Lucifer was up, off the Earth, where He committed a crime before He was sent down, to the Earth, away from the sight of God.

God wants us to understand that in the book of Genesis, He did not describe the location of what He called the garden. Still, He described its greenness and showed how it hosts animals (including human beings), rivers, cities, and minerals. He said that based on these depictions, mankind chose to take them for physicality (things and places) they had known on earth before He gave the picture/design of the earth to Moses.

Now, he asks us a question in this technological period: Would you [a man living in a primitive village] be sure that the photo that someone from a developed country has shown you of a beautiful house with flowers, people sitting or standing inside and around the house, a car in the garage, and all other things depicted is truly a finished work or a paper design of what the person has in mind to do some time from now?

Would you actually be able to tell that there is something called "Technology" in the developed country that makes things look very real as opposed to physical existence if someone from that country who knows these things didn't tell you whether it is the paperwork of an architect or a finished house?

He said the contrast between what people believe from those depictions in the garden and what He later revealed to Ezekiel several years after Genesis was written is troubling today, so He has come to remove the veil.

SPECIAL ANNOUNCEMENT

Analogy of Judgment System

This announcement shall be official and binding on the entire world at the time (on the day, date, hour, minute, and second) that this book is published on the Internet and through bookstore distribution channels.

At such time, the Lord God shall begin a new day of recording the sins of the world, and the same shall serve as the boundary between the generation of all those who died before this book and the generation of all those who shall begin the hearing of the things contained in this book.

As has [previously] been written in this book, everything that happens in this world has its roots in the Spirit realm, and so has the court system of this world.

There is a law in our world called "Expo-facto Law," if I spelled it right. It states that no one should be held responsible for an act committed before a law was made to declare that act a crime.

In view of this, the Lord God has identified two generations of Israel: one is that group before the laws and repentance were preached, and the other is that after the laws had been announced and taught.

Similarly, this book, having been given to a Gentile (a non-Jewish), brings the whole world population into the shoes of the Jews.

Even though the Gentiles (all the people of the world who are not Jews) have heard about the laws given unto the Jews by the Almighty God, they have never officially participated in the work of the Spirit until now. Therefore, they have come under the direct spotlight of the Great God of all creations. This book is theirs; by this, they shall be held accountable to God.

Now, both the Jews and the Gentiles shall be divided into two major groups for judgment when the system of this whole world shall come to an end.

Those who didn't hear the laws read shall be tried in a lower Court (Say, the Magisterial Court), while the higher court shall try those who have listened to the laws (Say, the Supreme Court).

Four judges shall preside over the lower court in Heaven (The Four Spirits reporting to Jesus). Jesus shall not be there, but He shall receive their reports.

They shall convict some people and pardon some. Those whom the four judges shall pardon shall be referred to the highest Court, where Jesus shall preside as Attorney along with the Great God (Chief Judge), but those convicted by the four judges shall be sentenced directly to hell (call it Prison/Jail).

Those found with lesser counts by the four judges and referred to the highest Court (to God Himself) shall be joined with those who have heard the laws for final judgment.

The purpose of referring people to the highest court is to allow the highest judge (God) to decide on the most difficult cases. [People facing judgment in Heaven shall not be physical bodies but the souls that are in our frames.]

God alone has the last authority to forgive or convict under difficult situations [His discretion to forgive is what the Christian book called His Grace, an undeserving forgivingness.]

This power of forgivingness (God's discretion) is what we call executive clemency in our human world. An executive clemency in our world is not deserving of any criminal but is a special privilege from the president to some convicted criminals. The grounds on which a president forgives some criminals are based on his/her personal view of each person's crime.

Court Judges do forgive some criminals as well by reducing their sentence terms after reviewing some circumstances surrounding a case.

An executive clemency was a power of authority exercised by Jesus when he forgave the sinner during his time of crucifixion.

That is why what preachers call 'deathbed confession' is wrong to administer since preachers are not God or Jesus to determine whether someone is qualified for God's forgiveness after the dying person has lived his/her entire life in sin. Those things the Spirit (God or Jesus) uses as determiners may not be applicable to the person. [Our tract or speaking time would explain the determiner/s.]

Also, there is a sin type constituting a difficult case for God, which is *Imposed Sin*.

Before now, the Bible has always been clear on *Intentional & Unintentional sins.* They are not difficult to judge, which is why they are those cases going to the lower court while the Imposed Sin goes to the higher court.

Under the Imposed Sin, God shall judge between a rape victim & the rapist, He shall judge between a subordinate & the boss, a soldier & the captive, a government & its people, an initiated person & the initiator, etc. [all these would be explained further through the publication of tracts and through speaking events].

King David (Israel's King who took the wife of his army general, Uriah, then later killed Uriah) and his types shall be judged in heaven under the imposed sin category.

Since He is God of All Knowing, He searches the innermost part of the heart to determine the motive behind every action.

After the final judgment, all convicted men and women shall be sent to prison (Hell), while those pardoned shall have a place of rest.

In the prison center, there shall be several divisions just as there are on earth; there shall be a perpetual gnashing of teeth for some (see this as a lifetime imprisonment with hard labor), while some may serve short-term sentences for other reasons God alone knows. End of Announcement.

God's Cycle of Destruction and Recreation of the World (Rapture-Resurrection-Judgment & New World)

These four biblical terms individually refer to the end of this corrupt system (this world) of Satan. They refer to a spiritual process of man's going to see God not in the physical body, man's facing judgment before God with His Son (Jesus), and the chosen ones receiving a new spirit on earth after judgment to live again; this time with Jesus in His New Kingdom on earth.

After listening to so many denominations, I got to know that not even one actually understands the connection of these four terms to explain the process of old-world destruction and new world creation by God.

The misunderstanding of these words is what makes the Jehovah's Witnesses, a denomination with a teaching coming close to the new world theory, argue with other denominations that the heaven (paradise) that the righteous shall live in is on earth, not anywhere else, but the others argue that the righteous shall leave this earth and go to live in Heaven with God forever.

Now that God has enlightened me more on this matter, it is my pleasure to share the truth with you, my fellow Christians.

The Rapture – is the first process of ending this ugly and corrupt system of things in this world.

It is a beautiful scene to see, but it is God's mystery that no man can easily understand or believe.

On that day people shall be as busy as they are always in their daily struggles. Then suddenly, the entire world system shall come to a standstill; everything shall stop moving, and all equipment wouldn't function anymore. No matter where you may be (whether on the Moon or on Mass, you must stop moving) and whatever you may be doing, you must stop doing it. Darkness shall fill the earth as the electric plants of every nation and its cities shall shut off.

Everyone everywhere in the world shall feel like they are sleeping and having a dream or seeing a vision. Then there comes a thunderous breeze (wind) blowing eastward accompanied by Lightning (flashes of light) that illuminates the world in a new glory. While the breeze sweeps the earth, then comes the resurrection.

The Resurrection- is the second process of ending the old world.

The resurrection shall be like everyone everywhere in the world; they shall be raised up to Heavens as the decayed bodies remain in dust and the physical bodies of those who were living before the rapture remain in their positions on earth. Those in beds shall remain so, and everyone shall hold his tools or bottles of beer in his hands as in the case of farmers and night clubbers, and every plane that flies shall stick in the air with all its crew, and everyone shall remain in his office as with government officials and all office workers.

This further means that the souls of both the dead and

the living before the standstill came shall be raised together. {The Soul (the second part of every human being, Thessalonians 5:23, which is an invisible part within the physical frame shall be raised to live in the Spirit realm to represent the decayed body that is lying in the tomb and the frozen body of anyone that was living before being caught in the rapture)} Then the judgment comes.

The Judgment- is the third process of ending the old world.

Then everyone (the Souls of all men and women) shall form one line, matching towards the Judgment Throne in Heaven.

There, people shall have a little memory of those that they knew in the past. The husband shall look at his wife and children and shall not know them, but with little memory that keeps him wondering inside himself as to where possible, he might have seen or known them but far little, he can ever believe knowing them, and the same they and every other person shall do. Everyone shall simply match on quietly looking onto the Judgment Throne.

Jesus will be there as the Attorney (a Lawyer or judge for the innocent), while God will be the main Judge, like a Supreme Court Judge. There shall be juries to be comprised of all the Angels God has been sending to earth to watch over mankind.

Then God shall separate those He found favorable in His own discretion from the wicked. Then, they shall be temporarily housed in Heavens for a period of time (maybe some hundred years) while the wicked shall be sent to the place prepared for them.

The Son of God (Jesus) shall work the earth (clean up) to make it ready for a new world while this temporary stay shall remain in place just like Moses remained in comma on top of Mount Sanai for several days as the angels of God took him on a tour in every part of the Heavens.

While the righteous (chosen ones) stayed temporarily in the rooms that Jesus had prepared ahead of judgment time, the New World gets underway.

The forming of the new world is the fourth process of ending the old world.

Finally, the souls of the righteous [those who found favor in the sight of God, not because they were very perfect but because of His special grace {God's method of grading people}] shall be restored to both the dust of the dead before the resurrection and to the frozen frames of those who were living before the rapture.

They shall gain a new life in which they'll know no more of their old world, while the bones of the wicked (those who became guilty in the sight of God) shall remain dead forever, for their souls have been taken to purgatory (the place of perpetual torment, call it Central Prison.)

Since the soul (spirit) doesn't die, so will the souls of the guilty ones remain in

Purgatory (jail) forever or for as long as God pleases.

. . .

Coming of the new King-then comes this moment when those who received new life shall receive the Son of man in His glory back to earth.

The same thunderous wind shall continue to sweep eastward while He descends to earth like a President landing in a helicopter while everyone shall see Him from every part of the earth in their states of having a vision. How this happens is like we do today as we watch a President on television from every part of the world we are.

The state of the new world shall be a marvelous one.

The new people shall not remember anything about a world that existed before and how that world worked because their souls have been renewed like the engine of an old vehicle has been washed off of dirty particles.

Jesus shall be their new King (President), and He shall appoint His own leaders everywhere around the world, and new laws and a new system of things shall be set in place.

The new world shall not follow the system of things that makes Satan's world wicked and corrupt today. It shall not have any man having personal possessions like we have today. That is, the new world shall be like the Kingdom of Heaven where no one owns anything; no marriage, no rich nor poor, no buying and selling, and no any other form of corruption. The new world shall not also know any form of jealousy/envy, and there shall be no wars. The new world shall know no boundaries for there shall not be Countries and different presidents, but Jesus alone shall be the world president while he shall appoint people to local positions like governors or superintendents today.

Wow, what a perfect world there shall be in those days! I want to be there!

How Much Time Left?

December 25, 2018@9:55pm Mankind shall live just less than a million years, but as for how close to or far away from a million years; that is the prerogative of the Almighty. Let those who have ears to hear, hear to do what is right while the time is yet to be.

The contrast between judgment and Jesus took our sins

I heard the Lord tonight, September 16, 2024@9:04 PM. He said judgment is a Spiritual requirement that awaits every man after this system has passed, while 'Jesus took our sins away' refers to a short-term condition on earth. It is compared to anyone forgiving a friend for a first-time offense to give the person the benefit of the doubt that he/she might not do it again. In Jesus's case, he promised to take a friend's sins away (forgive a Christian person's sins) 70x70 =4,900 times in a person's lifetime to allow the person to change to a better one.

The voice speaking to me as I write this portion tonight asked a question: If Jesus had died for mankind's sins and took them away so that mankind would be free, then why did the Bible say judgment awaits every man, and everyone shall be accountable to all the things he/she is doing in the world? If Jesus had taken all the sins away so that those who believe in him would not be condemned anymore, then why do we worry about Heavenly judgment?

How does Satan participate in human creation?

Have we ever wondered why God would give us a child who is disabled?

Some humans are born with conditions that make them incapable of doing anything for themselves, their parents, or God. Let's take a child born without knowing how to walk and talk.

So, when this story was given to me, the question that came out of the mouth of the spirit was: If the Bible is all true to God's word regarding the goodness of everything He made, then why would He allow His angels create someone who would bring suffering to his/her parents and even question his/her own existence?

Therefore, the spirit said God has nothing to do with causing unhappiness in children and their parents. He said that Satan is responsible for these things because He influences creation since He was one of the original angels (robots) of God.

Maybe someone in the science world would say certain drugs often cause some disabilities. To that assertion, the spirit would say: Who inspired the drugs? The source is traced back to Satan, who is behind the science of death in this world.

Things to do and not to do

In my school of the Spirit, I was taught many things about wrong and right things we do in our world.

This happened on Friday, July 5, 2024, at about 11:22 PM. My wife and I were having a bedtime prayer when the Spirit of God closed my mouth very tightly after I'd said God should forgive us our intentional and unintentional sins.

I was interrupted during this sacred moment. I was ready to listen because the Spirit of God had a message for me.

But after listening to the Lord's voice, I was reminded of previous messages, which is why I want to tell you what the Lord said to us.

1. Unintentional sins:

The Lord said I should have remained on saying He should forgive our unintentional sins alone because they're the sins we don't have any control over. They're sins of the spiritual forces that drive our emotions, such as anger, lust, fear, jealousy, envy, grudges, etc.

He said that with unintentional sins, God's discretion, called Grace, that is undeserving, shall waive some of them. For example, if anger propelled you so fast that you did something wrong even before you realized it, He shall look at it differently from the one you thought through before doing it under anger, lust, fear, jealousy, envy, grudges, etc.

2. Intentional sins:

The Lord said I shouldn't have said He should forgive our intentional sins because they're sins we think through before committing them.

He said they're grave because we have exercised our willpower to choose wrong and right.

I realized I needed a life change after hearing this message on July 5, 2024. So, I adjusted my intentional thoughts that I felt inside me as lust (L-u-s-t).

3. Deathbed Confession:

Deathbed Confession was one of several things I learned during my two-and-a-half years at the School of the Spirit.

God told all preachers not to request deathbed confessions because forgivingness is a special authority belonging to God alone.

When Jesus used it on the cross to forgive the sinner, he exercised his Heavenly authority and saw the sincerity in the sinner's confession, which was not made by compulsion (no one encouraged him to do so). Jesus looked into the man's heart to see the remorse, the regret, and the wish to have another time to change his ways.

Unfortunately, preachers cannot see inside a man's heart and determine his/her level of remorse, so they're unqualified to offer forgiveness to any man who has lived in sins all his/her life until the last moment.

However, anyone who wishes to correct his/her wrongs can do so before death. Such a turnaround attitude could help during judgment.

A wrong prayer

Also, during my school years, the Lord God told preachers to stop praying this way: May God grant you all your heart desires.

He said humans don't see people's hearts, so they cannot see the wrong and right desires of the people.

For example, among those hearts desiring prayers for business prosperity is a man who runs a mortuary. He desires more dead bodies to bring him more money. So, he is invoking the spirit of death to come upon the people. The question is: Is it God who approves these different kinds of death – motor accidents, knife stabbing deaths, and all immature deaths?

On the other hand, a person who is loving to a married person may want a prayer to separate a couple to enable him/her to marry the divorcee. The question is: Is it God who would approve of the separation?

So, why has every pastor been offering wrong prayers when he/she prays for all the heart desires?

Power of nudity/nakedness

The Lord God Almighty had shown me the power of nakedness during my school years.

He said if it was appropriate for mankind to remain naked to walk nude, then He shouldn't have clothed the original man in the Garden, even after the man had sinned against Him, God.

He spoke against the human practice of walking nude or

half-nude. He defined nakedness (nudity) as not having on clothes entirely, as well as any partial covering of the body exposing sexuality.

God said He made sexual organs to work in coordination with the senses of the eyes.

This secret is popular in the spirit world, so the Spirit women use it more to conquer the men who started everything and see women as useless in society.

That is why a woman would wear a specific garment at bedtime to catch her husband's or boyfriend's attention if he was not paying attention to her. That is why a woman would intentionally dress in a certain way to catch the attention of every man who is looking for sexual pleasure.

On the other hand, mankind's body stature has a profound impact on the senses of the eye. That is why every woman or man feels attracted to some parts of a man or a woman. Some people are attracted to the fat body of the opposite sex, while some people are attracted to the lean or slim body of the opposite sex. Still, some people are attracted to the genital look of other people.

So, in 2013, when I saw Westerners lying and walking half-nude on the beach in Miami, Florida, USA, particularly with women wearing their beach wear panties, cutting all in their butts, the Spirit descended on me to give me a complete understanding of nakedness (nudity).

He concluded by asking: "If a man's wife's bedroom nakedness can turn him on and vice versa, then how is it necessary to show the same body publicly?"

So, can you see how wrong things have become right things?

This story focuses on women for two major reasons: (1) Spirit women are in control of human sex activities in these last days, and (2) see what human women do with their bodies these days on the internet, where they often expose their sacred (God given) parts openly; see what they do with the body in the name of modeling, when they strip naked, leaving a tiny piece of clothing to cover just the sacred part; and see what they do with the body when they're dancing by rubbing their buttocks on men partners' wire rods.

Everything you see is an indoctrination of men into the women's world to control the minds of men in the human world, and it's a conquest that the women's spirits celebrate each year.

In the Spirit World, the Spirit women have a festival of conquest they celebrate every December to honor and rejoice over how they conquered the men's world.

To whom the power of the tongue belongs?

In the Bible, there is a saying that "life and death lie in the power of the tongue."

God revealed to us that this refers to the physical nature of the Bible.

The Bible's portion refers to the good or evil people do to anyone based on what the person says. It is a warning to everyone to beware of what they say because whatever comes out of their mouth could be used to judge or bless them by their fellow humans.

Therefore, the statement "Life and death lie in the power of the tongue" belongs to human beings who like or dislike others just by what comes out of their mouths, regardless of how Satan manipulated the tongue to plunge the person into trouble.

Moreover, whenever anyone places a swear or curse on another, that person is surrendering the other under the judgment of the gods of our lands.

God's judgment is one, and it comes only when the world ends, but the punishments people get while alive come from the gods of their lands. This means that the gods of each tribe or people always watch over them to monitor their behaviors and act upon any complaints against their people.

The Bible also reports these godly activities (activities of the lower gods) as ordinances of the Big God since He delivered mankind into Satan's hands at the time of man's rebellion in the Garden. This means that there are some statements in the Bible concerning laws and the breaking of the rules, such as don't eat this and that, don't do this and that.

In such a situation, any pronouncement of consequence is not of God since He (God) doesn't punish us many times, except the one punishment that awaits our souls after judgment in Heaven at the end of this ugly system.

Remember, God threw man out of the Garden along with Lucifer. Since then, Lucifer, now Satan, has been instituting His own laws and prosecuting people under their local laws.

Characteristics of the righteous and the unrighteous

So, many people have asked the question: Who will be the righteous person since the Bible says, "All have fallen short of the glory of God, or no one is righteous?"

Therefore, God has given me the answers.

Answers: He said the *righteous* would be the ones with limited dirt to clean after the judgment in Heaven, and the *unrighteous* would be the ones clogged with so much dirt in their souls.

This means righteous people are sinners, too, like the unrighteous people, but the righteous have a few sins in them, unlike the unrighteous, who enjoy sins so much that they have no limitations.

A further explanation of the righteous ones would take us to the story of King David. He was contaminated with sexual urges that made him always fall into sexual sin, but God still loved him for a reason we would reveal later.

Still, in David's story, we will learn how God would judge him and Moses and compare their Heavenly rewards.

What is yawning?

Let me use yawning for [your] case study on sneezing, coughing, fatting, and others to explain what a single act we carry on involuntarily means. But before I provide my personal version of the training that I received in the School of the Spirit, let me bring in what researchers say yawning is.

It goes like this:

"Sure, a yawn is a very natural reaction to a night of restless sleep, a boring work meeting, a traffic jam after a particularly long day at the office, or a response to another person's yawn. However, researchers have long pondered the yawn and the exact cause. Many assume yawning occurs from lack of oxygen, boredom, or sleepiness. However, scientists have always suspected that yawning has more to do with than just emotions alone."

From this discussion, I came to let you know that there are so many things about nature that even human science cannot find answers to, even though they [scientists] often come close.

Since we live in the science world now, let's see what scientists say yawning is: A **yawn** is a reflex consisting of the simultaneous inhalation of air and the stretching of the eardrums, followed by an exhalation of breath. **Yawning** (oscitation) most often occurs in adults immediately before and after sleep, during tedious activities, and as a result of its contagious quality.

In addition, different regions of the brain control yawning and breathing. Still, low oxygen levels in the paraventricular nucleus (PVN) of the hypothalamus of the brain can induce yawning.

Another hypothesis is that we yawn because we are tired or **bored**.

Now let's discuss one thing from the scientific definition, and that is "Low oxygen." Science says oxygen is "a chemical element found in the air as a colorless, odorless, tasteless gas that is necessary for life."

So, this brings our discussion to one point where science says, "certain gas of the air," and religion says "other group of Spiritual forces" [all being called "Air"] often cuts down in the body while another comes into the body.

Still, as the world ponders over the exact meaning of yawning, they say it is due to being tired [hypothesis]. Tiredness is the loss of energy, while energy remains the name of some forces of the air that leave the body due to different conditions; it could be the lack of food, water, or the puncher of the body [injury].

Therefore, in the following explanation, you [my reader] shall come to know exactly that yawning is the exchange [coming in and coming out] of two groups of Spiritual Forces that go into man's body to work there.

So ride with me to get the correct answer to nature [God's invisible work]:

Yawning [opening the mouth wide to let air in & out] is the perfect way to understand the outing and entering of two large groups of spirit workers that come to earth to perform duties in our bodies. For example, all the night spirits that go into man's body [there {like all company workers do to go to work in one big bus in our world} break up into different units to do other and related jobs such as a unit to effect sleep, a unit to cause dreams, a unit to defend the body, including those that squeeze the heart to contract to pump blood to all parts of the body {just like human beings do when they squeeze a rubber pump to inject liquid into human body} and, all others that cause all muscular {involuntary} movements that take place in all living things {plants and animals}].

So, when a man [for example] needs to get out of sleep at night, an internal alert is given to all concerned so that a large group [those who are not related to Light at all] has to rush out of the body to be replaced by (a) semi-light group [if it was still night time wake up for peeing purpose {even the spirits to cause that contraction to force water out of the body come in}] or (b) daylight group [if it was daybreak time wake up for daily activities {even the spirits that enable walking come in too while the spirits that help every man to lie down leave along with others}].

Therefore, what every man experiences on earth in the form of yawning is a forceful [instantaneous] exchange of duties between two large groups of workers operating in the Spirit realm.

We often notice this kind of exchange, primarily when we're hungry, sleepy, or tired. That is what we call 'yawning' that takes place [when hungry] because certain spirits uphold the body when there is no food [that group comes in] while certain spirits help with food digestion [cause contraction process] and they must leave too. [When sleepy] all the quiet related spirits come down to work. And when we say 'quiet spirits,' we mean forces of the air that are not violent with human beings in their duties but violent in their world so that we see some of them fight wars or participate in races [ride cycles or drive cars] in our dreams. And [When tired] all the violent spirits [spirits that enable every man to strike hard] begin to decrease [leave the body] to be replaced by weaker [man says "lazy"] spirits. This decrease in stronger spirits being replaced by weaker ones leaving and coming in very large groups [just like factory workers do in our world today on an hourly basis to change shifts] results in the mouth opening very wide and the nasal cavity contracting to let out and let in air [by definition of human science] or let in Spiritual Forces [by definition of religion {the belief in the unseen powers}].

Now, there is a relationship between hunger and tiredness, so one may see the relationship between the forces that act together.

Special offer (forgiveness of sin)

What does it mean when the Bible says Jesus shall

forgive us our sins [while alive] when we confess our sins?

When Jesus told us to believe in His name and confess our sins because He is faithful and just to forgive us, He meant that if anyone sins, that person has caused an enmity (a barrier) between himself and Christ or the Spirit of God. It means the free flow of the good ones to the person has been impeded, but when he/she confesses, then the veil is removed, and peace for communication returns again.

However, one thing that happens in the Spirit realm is that a record is kept for that offense to wait for judgment day.

This is similar to what happens on earth when two individuals quarrel and can't speak freely to each other while they yearn for peace. So, to remove the barrier between them, the offender apologizes (confession), and the offended accepts (forgiveness), but the offended shall never forget (erase) the incident in his/her heart, even if he/she says it's forgotten.

Therefore, telling someone that grievous things can be forgotten is one of the lies of the heart. Though new memories might cover the old, the old remains buried deep inside. Isn't it true about the heart?

Therefore, preachers have never understood the two words (*Spiritual* and physical) involved in what Jesus said. Spiritually, we shall still be held accountable for all we do while alive because there is a record in Heaven for each of us until judgment day. Physically, we're required to make peace with the Lord [apologize] for every wrong we commit that can impede the free flow of His power to us on earth.

Still, by this wrong interpretation of the word of God, many Christians find comfort in the commission and confession of Intentional sins daily.

The Narrow Gate:

Here is a list of a few things to measure the narrow gate. [Why will only a few be chosen?]

a. **The little gods we serve:** [Beginning from every man's heart] any specific purpose for attending church becomes a person's god that he/she serves as compared to the Almighty God he/she goes to serve. For example:

a.1. Some people go to church to get access to material things the church offers [every other service to God is just a show].

a.2. Some go to get a girlfriend or a boyfriend [every other service to God is to impress that person]

a.3. Some go to get the handsome or beautiful pastor or choir member [every other service to God there is to impress that person].

a.4. Some pastors work for material benefits they get or will get [the good preaching and all the service to God there is to lure members to give].

a.5. Some people choose to be pastors because they pre-empt the material benefits, the honor they'll get, and the women they will access [there are more men pastors than women today]. When you subtract these benefits, the person finds commitment to church service meaningless.

a.6. Some use magical powers [wonders workers] to attract members and glorify their honor [this becomes the person's god].

b. **Your heart matters, not your service:**

b.1. God will take the money you obtain cruelly and give it to the church so that society will call you a kind person, but He (God) knows that you're boastful, proud, and arrogant. Your unclean money will take care of the same people your actions affect negatively [maybe you're a corrupt government official whose actions deny health benefits, cause hunger, and other unfortunate conditions that reduce some people in the community to sufferings and beggars; the church can still use your money to take care of them].

b.2. God takes the money you bring from prostitution, robbery, or killing to help those in need, but He (God) sees your heart as one that devours people.

b.3. God is happy when you offer to the person [most often women] in need but He (God) sees the heart of yours that gives it if that heart is to lure the woman to bed or to entrap the man to your commands as a subject to you, God sees all that.

C. **The decisions you make cause more harm than good:**
c.1. The word of God, through His son Jesus, has already made it clear that nations will be judged on the day of judgment in Heaven [Christian nations are very much aware of this] which means the decisions of their governments have the propensity to acquit or convict the nation during judgment time in Heaven. But how will God acquit or convict a whole nation that is full of good and bad people? Well, that is

going to be a separate judgment of all those leaders who took those decisions [dealing with them regime by regime and time by time] during the lifetime of that nation.

So, are your decisions to kill, to free, to prosecute, to convict, to allow, to make and all of what leaders do for or to people harmful more than being helpful?

How does God keep a record of all things?

Luckily, this world [the period of these things God has given me to write] is living in the computer stage when the information storage system is simple to manage. The computer age has produced a chip system [a very tiny component] capable of holding/hiding large amounts of information [scripts, voices, and images] that can be retrieved at any time they need to be seen.

So, when the word of God says God keeps a record of all we do in this world. At the same time, we're alive, it is simply reporting a computer storage system in Heaven, and that means God has been storing everything that is happening in this world country by country, tribe by tribe, and person-by-person until the last day of human existence before the judgment day comes in Heaven.

As I was writing the computer chip example Spirit gave me, I remembered something else: the ADT security camera system I have in my house. The camera records every movement in and around my house. The camera has a way I can view past activities to see who entered my house or who came to my door and what the person did. I can view everything on the camera anytime I want to do so. Also, through the camera system, I can be anywhere in the world to look inside my house and around the entrance.

So, reflecting on what the Spirit told me, I believe that some things in the Bible represent technological terms in the Spirit realm. I believe that God is truly keeping an eye on everything we do in the world and keeping a record of all of it. He will surely show us proof of our deeds in the world.

What is God's Grace?

The first example of His grace was demonstrated by His son, Jesus, while on the Cross of Calvary. Jesus [for some reasons known by him alone] decided to wave the sins of the criminal waiting on the other side to be hanged. This is just like a president issuing an executive pardon to someone convicted of a specific crime. While it is easy to determine the reasons behind a president's decision on earth, it is not easy for man to do so on the part of God because only He [God] knows what to put together to derive grace mathematically.

What is God's mathematics of sins?

Let's take this scenario in which a man's number of sins is computed against his number of goods and divide the total sum by two, then add the man's daily heartburn against the evils he does [man will call it his remorse/regrets], then subtract his joy over the things he does wrongly [man will call it his wicked (unrepentant) heart that keeps him doing them repeatedly] plus other things not disclosed to me.

Hey, have you ever seen or heard two people discussing

the manner of evil they committed a moment ago? One jumps here and there with a rejoicing voice about how he did what he did and how he loves to do it again and again. At the same time, the other sits sadly, regretting his action and refusing to repeat a similar thing.

Tell me, if a president had to listen to the case of these two to decide on granting executive pardon, which of these two deserves it?

I believe in myself [I, the storyteller] that the one with such remorse was either lured (enticed, persuaded) into the action against his inner will [that inner will is the spirit that God had put in him, which is constantly battled by Satan's spirit inside him also] or forced (commandeered) into doing it. So, to me, he deserves to be given a second chance to return to his community and family. It happens with God, too.

So, you see, why we all are sinning each day, and we believe in the grace of God to save us from our sins, we can never tell how that grace can be earned. That is why it's wrong to keep assuming that God is faithful and just enough to forgive us [All] our sins. That's why it is important to avoid committing intentional sins as much as possible in your life and focus on the things of God.

It is also good [at a certain point in one's life] to stop doing wrong things [that thing everyone knows by his/her conscience] and begin to do good before his/her death comes; that way, the room is going to be opened wide for the person to be forgiven of those unintentional sins he/she may commit or may have committed [plus, he/she can also avoid committing the 3rd sin category called the Imposed

Sin (an action by which some people commandeer others)].

Where did the rich and poor come from?

Often, some people regret to have been born into poverty, and they say when they die, they shall not go unto poor man and woman again. For black Africans and [perhaps] other races, they say they shall be born into the white race because they think the white race is superior and rich.

But who has ever chosen where to be born? Who was there when he/she was manufactured into a human being? No one has control over that. God did not make any man poor; neither did he make any man rich.

Let me tell you this: God hears all these accusations against Him, and that's why He sent me to clarify what is happening in the world.

He says He made every man equal. He provided everything [the resources of the earth] free for all. He [having come down as Jesus] taught the people [his disciples] how to do things in the world; he exemplified to them how to live together, how to abandon owning property, how to abandon chasing after riches of the world, how to share together and how to work together for the enjoyment of all [and that was socialism and communism/communality].

God says Satan is the architect of the order of this world today. Satan is the one using a divide-and-rule system by introducing an ownership system into the world of human beings, and yet he (Satan) makes some rich [in fact, those with hard hearts are the easiest to work with] while he suffers most of the people who for some reasons waver all the time that makes it hard for him to work consistently with them and for some, it is due to the sins of their ancestors who may have failed their duties to appease Him (Satan) at some point in time, yet for some, poverty is Satan's way of punishing them for some reasons he knows, opposite to the way God uses His Grace [discretion] to save some people out of certain sins.

How this happens is that Satan, through His demons (the ancestral spirits of each family line), is in the habit of denying other people the abundance of things of this world through several means that take away money or, in the pre-money era, was unproductivity.

In this money era, He breeds in sicknesses into families, He breeds in troubles, He breeds in bad habits like drunkenness or smoking or extreme sexual desires; all of which drain out money and at the same time land people into trouble. He even breeds in instability of the mind so that people get weary of doing certain things that they think would bring them more money. As they keep changing from one thing to another, they get caught up in other unfavorable conditions and continue to be down.

Thus, instability [shifting and shifting] is a general condition that the world's largest population suffers so that they keep away from achieving wealth/more money. Those who achieve wealth in this world know this phenomenon.

Therefore, you men, stop accusing God of disparities that you find among yourselves. He is fair in all things.

The untold story of Abraham and his wife, Sarah

- The story of Abraham and his wife is clear evidence of how ancient men used cultures and traditions against women. Still, these abuses were left unreported in the Bible because men were the custodians of their practices, and they (men) wrote the Bible. [By way of men's cultural practices, Jesus's mother was abused as well].

- Ancient cultures and traditions considered women to be properties of men, and so did Sarah to Abraham.

- So, Abraham initially believed in his heart that he had a beautiful wife whom he could trade for food. That was why he carried her along even when he knew the king could take her away from him. [Who would take his beautiful wife to a King's palace if Kings were in the habit of killing men to take their wives? Why would Abraham take his beautiful wife along in the first place, then later decide to hide her true relationship with him? So, God being God who sees our hearts, saw Abraham's heart before they set out on the journey].

- Therefore, God saved Sarah from the barter system of men selling their wives or daughters for riches. Thus, God knew Abraham's deceitful heart's desire to trade his wife for a favor. That was why God saved Sarah from the King's abuse.

- Unfortunately, since men were the custodians of everything in ancient times, including writing and reporting events, they didn't look at Abraham's sin; rather, they concentrated on God's miraculous work of saving Sarah.

Some things for some people, but everyone can learn (A Call for African Development Model)

Come, let us lament Africa. Come, let us cry for this humankind. Oh, Africa, how low you've become!

The God of everyone came to earth for the first time and landed in the Mesopotamia region, now the Middle East, where He has been doing many things worldwide. Still, mankind has not been seeing them because mankind has been programmed that God completed His work in Israel when, in a true sense, God had just started.

Behold, the Hebrews, now Israelites, were a segment of the middle-colored people of Asia He chose to start His work with before moving on to other peoples. That's how, in December 2005, He sent His Spirit to Africa, where the black humans, the last of three human colors in Heaven, live. From there, one of them was chosen to bring them messages concerning things of the Heavens and of the earth.

This man of their kind has a special message for them, but whether they would listen to him is a different matter altogether.

The message from God for Africans is that 'Africa should

adopt a new development model' that is different from that of Western and Asian nations.

God warned Africans not to enter military pacts with the Western world or invest in the military; instead, they should invest in infrastructure and technology to help them develop Africa for the world's future.

God said the Western world and Asia have invested heavily in the military and are competing over technology superiority so much that one day, they would use the same technology to destroy each other.

So, God said since Africa has not been militarized yet, African leaders should unite their voices in opposition to arms manufacturing in Africa.

God said Africa must be the free land to which people fleeing wars would run one day from all over the world to seek safety.

God said African leaders must say no to every developed country that wants to militarize Africa. Thus, Africans must stand their ground and tell everyone that they want their partnerships and economic and technological development.

Similarly, God said Western nations must stop militarizing the world. God said the arms race around the world is caused by Western countries' desire to control and suppress other races in the world. God said if there weren't the desire for control and suppression through the terror of the gun from the West, there wouldn't be any need for other nations to choose arms manufacturing. There wouldn't be the desire to protect oneself from Western domination.

God said the desire by Western nations to bring peace to the world using guns in new and dangerous forms today would never bring peace, except hostility and wars because the nation destroyed today would come back tomorrow with the desire for revenge.

I was told during school that the root causes of conflicts worldwide are the desire of one nation or group to change all the humans in the world to become what the group is.

It is the desire to democratize the whole world, spread one language and culture throughout the world, cheat and steal from other people, become greedy by amassing wealth upon wealth without letting others prosper, and break down nations to find new business opportunities.

Above all, it is the desire to use God's word, the Bible, to wage wars to defend God. It is the desire to replace God's word, the Bible, with human rights laws. And it is the desire to abandon Him, God, to worship the things of the world, which are the properties of the other god.

Africa, listen to the Spirit. Stop listening to your oppressors and be independent in your thinking about yourself. Stop the one-idea mentality that has kept you down for centuries. Africa, make bold policies that can suffer you in the short term but uplift you in the long term. The choice you make today will determine your long-term future.

This ministry is ready to answer questions about this topic.

Africa needs science and technology

By the time the Bible was inspired, the Heavens were well advanced already, just like the earth is in the 21st century. But to be exact, the Heavens were ten times more advanced than our times because we're about to use robot humans to do our work.

God was already using robot angels to do His work in Heaven, which is why the Bible contains passages such as, "God said, come let us make man," "Then God said, let there be light, and there was light," "God took six days to create the earth, and He rested on the seventh day," "God has record of everything," etc.

These passages represent God's wisdom in revealing heavenly science. They explained how quickly everything was done and how sophisticated Heaven is.

Imagine how vast our universe is and all the things in it. Still, it took just six days to create them all. That explains how technology works faster compared to ancient times when man used his hands to do every piece of work.

So, when God says He will destroy the world, He is simply revealing that He has the most sophisticated technology that can smash everything in one second. It is like the United States would tell the world that they're capable of using nuclear bombs to destroy a whole nation in a few hours.

So, the science of the Spirit world is the mortarboard of the human science we see today. It is for all heavenly dwellers. All the angels know science. It is a universal gift to them all because it is useful to all.

We all remember the Bible saying humans were made in God's image. In the statement, the truth is that whatever God designed for the Heavens is what He designed for the earth. That's why He created every human with the knowledge of creation. We were all born with the sense of making things, which is called human science.

That's why history tells us that there were different civilizations worldwide. Every group of people knew how to make things for themselves.

In Africa, people had their blacksmiths to make tools and weapons. They had people to make clay pots and dishes. There were weavers to make clothes. They had healers.

All of these were available in Africa even before the Europeans arrived.

So, why did Africans leave behind? Why didn't they grow their sciences? Why did they abandon their God-given talents?

There is only one word that the Spirit revealed to me – *complacency*.

After my professors explained all these things to me one after another, the last professor said Africans became complacent after the Europeans arrived with their goods.

He said Africans were too quick to take an interest in foreign goods, so they abandoned all their trades. They desired European-made goods so much that they neglected their locally produced items.

This led to European domination of the African continent. This encouraged Europeans to label Africans as lazy people.

Unfortunately, Africans cannot participate in the technology competition, which creates jobs and better lives for Westerners today.

But God said the time had arrived for Africa to receive

science and technology. He said Africans must prioritize science and technology for their development purposes. He said they must reject arms manufacturing right now and focus on building the necessary infrastructures that every developed country has so that one day, even Western citizens would find life easier in Africa when wars break out in their homelands.

But he said while Africans are embracing technology transfer from those who already have technology, they must also invoke the development of their local sciences. This means Africans must organize their local sciences, too, to grow them formally.

At this juncture, the Spirit told me that what Africans usually reject and call evil is not as evil as they consider it in Africa. That was when the Spirit told me to tell Africans that Western people didn't abandon everything they knew from ancient days, except that they modernized (upgraded) them in what they call a scientific way today.

The Spirit told me to look at everything science has produced to illustrate what they were saying clearly. Is there no science that kills and no science that heals? Are the heal and kill sciences not the same as good and evil? So, He asked: Why is African science alone evil? What's about the African science of joining fractured bones? And many other good sciences.

What happened to your gods?

Firstly, let's understand what the small (g) gods are.

They're the children of the Big (G) God, whose name is

all over the earth. He would call them His angels (formerly angles) or His extensions.

That's why He uses them to reach out to every part of the Heavens and the earth. They're called small (g) gods because they share the same characteristics as Him, unlike us humans. He is a Spirit, and so are they. He is a changeable being, and so are they. He can make Himself small, large, long, short, fluid, fly, walk, crawl, break apart, and reassemble, and they can do the same.

God is everything that man sees in this world, and the angels are His extensions, doing all He does through them.

We told a story about the functionality of the electric generator. We said it is one unit that produces electric energy, which works through different mediums to produce different results. We said the electric energy would enter a machine called a refrigerator to make water cold or harden it into solid, just the same way the electric energy would go on to another machine called an air conditioner to turn hot air into cold air, the same energy would go to a light bulb to produce light in a dark place, and on and on.

So, in the Heavens, God is that one power-producing unit that works through the different angels He made to produce different results, which we see in the Heavens and the earth.

As we said earlier, angels have the same capabilities as God, which is why they're called the small (g) gods.

Well, the analogy we just gave portrays God and the spirits as machines, but it's a different ball game when it comes to them being living beings like humans.

As living beings, God and His angels can think and make

decisions. They can create and destroy what they create. That's how we have different models of things in the Heavens and the earth.

They have an organized way of doing things, which is called their government system. But as we know, the Bible tells us that a conflict broke out in Heaven, and a second group of angels began to do things on their own. This group established themselves outside the Headquarters, often referred to as Heaven. They formed their government system alongside what God has. And they began ruling mankind alongside their father—God.

So Satan, their king, has one archangel, after whom he has appointed four from the angels who broke away from God with Him and made the four to be local authorities over the earth's four corners.

These four great demons are Satan's archangels of superior authorities above all demons. They are strictly accountable to Satan through Alassaman, Satan's immediate angel.

Satan governs the earth through the four demons. This is the original government system of the demon world, from which other powers began to emerge as the earth's human population grew.

Difference between Satan's and God's activities

Well, just as God gave the angels some freedom, called autonomy, to do things on their own, that's how Satan gave autonomy to His own, but His autonomy is not as free as

God's system is. He monitors His servants very closely, unlike God's open system.

The reason is apparent: He, Satan, exploited God's open system to break away from God. God didn't like it, but the way He set up His system made it impossible to reverse it at the time.

So, these gods established the systems, cultures, *and traditions* every society has today. Each god would capture a human being to speak to him and give instructions on how people should live, and these rules would become the ways of life for the people.

They created special circles of administration, which would become oracles or temples where people went to hear from the gods or get solutions to problems. This is how the earth was ruled before Christianity came.

Before the emergence of Christianity, these gods had taken over the entire world and had chosen some people who would become their mediums of administration. These were called the chosen ones. Among them are mediums of making songs - singers, mediums of healing, mediums of creation - scientists, mediums of finding out - seers, mediums of giving -helpers, mediums of destruction – killers and sickness givers, and so on.

This system was programmed to grow with every generation. It is called destiny, so each man's generation would continue to produce people to do these things in the ways the gods deemed fit.

But this system was interrupted when Christianity came. Christianity condemned the ways of the gods, saying everything about them was evil, so people who were supposed to serve these gods began to abandon them to go to church. These oracles they worshipped were left in ruins because every child was taught not to worship or listen to their gods anymore.

That's why some of these gods slowed down their activities and began to recalibrate their ways.

It would be shocking to learn the result of their recalibration, and it would be a challenge to understand why so many things are happening in God's name today. [We may not be able to write everything people need to know in our books, which is why we shall publish tracts and host speaking events as time passes].

Why do the gods need sacrifices?

Sacrifices are gifts to the spirits. The spirits need them for survival because they are food for them. God Himself needs food, so He made humans work the earth to provide it.

But to understand the issue of gifting to the spirits, let's start with why God made the earth and put us humans on it to work.

Throughout our teaching, we continue to say that the earth is a replica or second copy of the Heavens. Everything on earth is available in the Heavens, but what is in the Heavens is very soft, so it has less energy. It is like comparing natural food to genetically prepared food today.

This replication of the Heavenly resources for the earth is reported in the Book of Genesis. The book has verses about trees, minerals, animals, water, fish, and so on, but these reports bear names of the things on earth, which is why the people couldn't understand Genesis. They saw it as the earth itself, Moses drew.

In my book, *Interpretation Fourth*, I drew how food processing takes place in the Spirit realm.

Right now, what is happening in this 21st century between technology countries and naturally rich resource countries is the perfect example of the relationship between the Heavens and the earth.

Technologically advanced countries want to switch from carbon-rich fuel energy to clean energy, so they need the minerals necessary to produce clean energy for themselves. That's why they're going to Africa and other areas where they can extract these resources. They must have a good relationship with these places to get their needs. They don't have to like the people, but they need that business relationship to get their needs satisfied.

So, the reason God made the earth was to harden the things of Heaven to store more energy in them. That's why the trees of Heaven became hard on earth. The minerals and everything in Heaven, including humans, were hardened on earth.

So, there is more energy stored in the earth's crust than in Heaven. The energy is not only abundant but is stronger. One unit of the earth's energy can do a lot in Heaven.

Now, you may be wondering how God gets the energy from the earth. The answer is He gets it through us humans.

We, humans, are God's machines, complex machines that do many things for Him. This means we're made of many simple machines that work together to accomplish God's mission on earth.

The hand is a simple machine capable of holding, cutting, lifting, cleaning, crushing things, etc. That's the work of one simple part of God's robot machine.

Inside the human body, this big machine, are other parts that ground things, change things, store things, and do many other things for God.

So, we humans are here on earth to process the different kinds of energy God needs by eating the grass, the animal, the bird, the fish, and drinking the water. The water sends these food types to our bodies, which host the energies that are available in the soil containing these minerals or energies God needs.

Thus, when we eat food, the energy we receive from it is stored in different parts of our body, but the largest quantity of it is deposited into our blood, bone, and semen (the sexual fluids of humans).

Let's not forget that the angels are like God, so they also need the same energies God needs. But now, there is a break-away group of angels. They would start to misuse energy. God had to find another way to protect what He needed. This is where the splitting of energy came from. Thus, the terms 'clean' and 'unclean' came about. God would prefer to protect the clean energy produced deep within the body and leave the unclean energy to the angels since it is readily acces-sible. This is the difference between blood and semen (human sexual fluid).

So, God would issue a decree that mankind should not have sex from one person to another since it would weaken the layers built around the sex organs that would give easy access to the breakaway angels. This means as we have sex from one person to another, we're exposing ourselves to satanic invasion of our sexual fluids. Our sexual fluids would become polluted by the forces God would call maggots.

Satan and His men were deemed the pollutants or maggots because they would bring dirt into the system God made to feed from. That's why God stopped receiving His energy from human blood, rather, He would receive it from the semen and would say mankind must not move from one man or woman to another to create stability in the semen that wouldn't pose difficulties in the way of His transport angels, who come to earth daily to enter the human body to take the energy from the body to Heaven to keep it running.

Now, this brings us to why Satan kills too much.

As I said earlier, today, our world is discussing green energy as a replacement for fossil energy. This is happening because human science has reached the stage of knowing how many pollutants are in fossil fuels compared to the minerals used for green energy production.

So, in Heaven, God knows how much dirt is in blood since it is directly under the skin and can be infused with many things from the outside when a man gets a cut on the skin. That's why it takes so much work to remove impurities from it and get it clean. After removing impurities, there is almost nothing left to feed on to run the system in Heaven. That's why more blood is usually needed to get a certain quantity that is good to power a system in the Spirit realm. That gives us the answer as to why Satan kills more to get more blood to process to get the energy He and His collaborators need.

The same is true with the human flesh or any other

human part used for a sacrifice. They are polluted and contain less quantity of the energy needed to run a system in the Spirit realm.

Giving sacrifices to the spirits

The practice of offering a sacrifice to a spirit, called libation, is rooted in trading.

The word "Trading" is very much associated with Satan more than with God since God would offer rewards such as promotions based on faithfulness or commitment to Him. At the same time, Satan would set conditions for a promotion or for an offer of more power to His underservants.

The difference between giving to God and Satan is that God wants it to be done willingly, called cheerful giving, while Satan puts a demand in place. Satan would say: This is what you must bring or do before I give you what you want.

So, if anyone has the good spirit in him/her but puts a demand in place to exercise that gift, then he/she is doing it Satan's way, which is why he/she shall be judged by his/her intents or reason of using God's power.

So, as we delve into this story, let's focus the topic on how Satan uses the word trade in His enclave.

When Satan and His men came down from Heaven, He established a system He called the *Homage System*. He required His underservants to visit Him yearly and report to Him all their works, but He also required gifts from each servant.

He assessed the gifts (something deeper to explain exclusively) and gave them the gifts of powers in exchange for the value He attached to every gift. This system explains why one oracle can destroy another oracle and why the gods of our lands compete against one another.

Also, this explains the scientific competition mankind finds in this world, particularly the science of weapon manufacturing.

All other competitions in this world are also based on this since other lower powers oversee the little things we call crimes, trickery, and anything unholy.

Before I was told about all this, the Spirit of God had to first school me physically in this.

One early morning in 2008, I woke up from bed in a strange condition. My neck was stretching like a duck would stretch its neck continuously, and my head was twisting from side to side as a duck would. [I wish I could be on television to demonstrate exactly how it happened to me].

I was a bit terrified, but quickly, I reminded myself of how the Spirit had been dealing with me for over a year now. The Spirit had the habit of demonstrating things to me physically before a voice would come to explain what the happening represented.

So, I waited.

For about two days, my family cried because they thought my condition was getting worse. They thought that I was not only crazy (insane), but I was also coming up with a sickness that no one would explain.

But on the second day, the voice came down on me to reveal that it was the practical demonstration of a spiritual attack that would cause someone to become crippled or deaf or blind or have epilepsy or something else with no logical explanation.

These things are happening scientifically under the gods of human science, so we can see situations like this given medical names and having medical solutions or no permanent solutions.

After the revelation, another spirit came with a message for a solution. He said one of my sisters should kill a duck to cook for me to eat alone, which would restore me. He said no other person should do this ritual except my sister (whose name I can't call now, but she's alive).

So, my family bought a duck quickly, and my sister did as was instructed. About an hour later, I was better.

So, he said, the duck was an offering or gift to the spirit. He said it was done this way to demonstrate in real life that the things happening to humanity, not limited to Africans alone, are the works of the spirits called the gods of our lands. He said these things happen in several ways according to races, kingdoms (countries), tribes, clans, and individual families.

Solutions are also provided differently from one kingdom or person to another based on the gods responsible for everyone's family lines.

Through this study of libation (giving to the gods for appeasement), I was able to understand the purpose of wars and their rewards.

Wars represent blood offerings to the gods. The one who kills more stands the chance of receiving more knowledge. He said that is why other countries are leading in knowledge in the world since they prioritized wars in all their endeavors.

He said the spirits know their hearts. He said they don't care about death because they're the willing souls of people who want to die anytime for whatever they want. He said it is one reason they have been blessed among mankind with abundant knowledge.

Knowledge grows faster in their lands because they're good at offering sacrifices to the gods of their ancestors.

Before I end this, let me say that the word "blessing" used in this story and in any similar way is the quasi-blessing abundant in this wicked world. That's why a man would kill to take another's possessions and say God has blessed him. Similarly, a prostitute would make money and say God has blessed her. This world has so many look-like blessings, but we would understand it better under the Information Super-highway.

How altars are made

In one of our stories, we discussed how Christianity displaced the gods of every ancient society.

Those whom the gods chose long before Christianity came were supposed to continue performing their duties, producing children who would take after them, but these children have all rebelled against their gods and have run to the church. They love the church, and it causes them to waiver all the time in front of their gods, so the gods are not able to use these new generations.

This caused the gods to recalibrate their attitudes towards the earth because they still loved their children. That's why they would arrest some of these children and use them to do good things since they're the gods of repentance. They're from the moderate group of the gods, so they would set up churches to administer God's goodness.

They're acceptable to God for as long as the mediums (humans) they use continue to obey the good side of God. The good side of God is to abstain from the misuse of the power of God.

Let's take a break to revisit the Bible. The Bible contains a passage about good and evil, put in a parable as the tree of knowledge of good and evil, found in Genesis 2:17.

In my school of the Spirit, I was told that this passage describes exactly what we see in the world of creation and destruction. It means that God has two major sides: one that creates or produces things and the other that destroys or breaks down that which was created. Applying these two makes the case of good deeds or bad deeds.

The application of good or bad starts with intent and ends with implementation. This means, from the start, what you want to do is an intent of why you're doing it and how you're doing it.

You may pretend to be doing good with no strings attached, but God knows from when you bore the intent in your heart. He would see why you intend to do what you're announcing to a person, or a group of persons, or the congregation, or the whole world, even before you start to implement your action.

So, you see why it is difficult to judge the works of the gods in the name of churches?

In one of our stories, we revealed that there are two opposing camps in the demon world; those called moderates are fixed on doing good things and are called the repentant spirits, while those called draconian women, or radical men are fixed on doing evil and are called the wicked forces. So, the moderates are always roaming about to do good deeds such as freeing the captives, healing the sick, counseling the broken hearts, feeding the hungry, and other things.

But these good-hearted spirits work through human mediums whose willpower directs them. A man's willpower is his/her ability to decide what he/she wants. So, a person's willpower directs every spirit towards what should be given to the person. This happens because spirits are automatic machines for God. They can be triggered to give sound knowledge or bad knowledge.

That is why every temple can do good or evil depending on what has been requested. It takes a different force to change the situation based on other inquisitions (requests of the heart).

Now, what is an altar?

An **altar** is any place or person prepared by a spirit for the purpose of administering through the place or person. There are great and low altars, but many people look at only the great ones, which is why they don't see the altar on which they were set.

Among the great altars are religious and scientific; among the low altars are singing, sex, greed, and other altars.

. . .

244

Religious altars are places of worship. A place of worship or communication with the spirit could be in a church setting or the traditional setting known as a shrine.

In the church setting, the spirit administers to some people through the seat or pulpit or floor or a piece of thing chosen to be the incanter (a new word the spirit gave me while writing this story today, July 10, 2024). An incanter is any physical thing used by a spirit to connect to a person.

Believe me, my wooden chair was used to demonstrate how material things are used for altars. [I could explain more about my chair during a speaking event].

A religious altar is most significant to our discussion because the religious world is divided. It is the altar on which all spiritual churches are based. They're mixed up with traditional altars pretending to be good ones but focusing on doing evil rather than good.

So, what are some examples of traditional altars? Traditional altars focus on worldliness while acting to be for God. They prioritize material gains as the secular/pagan world does.

Still, it is very difficult to distinguish the real church altars from the traditional altars since the human mediums these spirits use have turned their hearts to amassing wealth for themselves, which is why they would be judged based on their intents of whatever they do for people.

It is a question of how you used the power of God to free the captives. Was money your focus, or was setting the captive free your focus? If money was the focus of using the power the spirit administered through you, then money was the god that you served, and the same you corrupted the work of the spirit with since you demanded money to be paid before using God's power to set the captive free of disease or anything else.

Even those churches calling themselves the good ones shall be judged based on the same intent. Did you do all the preaching for God or for the money and honor and other things you received? If the benefit is greater than the humble heart, then you have corrupted God's name.

In other stories, we shall talk about singing, sex, greed, and other altars.

Food poisoning and prevention

There are accusations of witchcraft in Africa. Africans speak so loudly about witches and wizards. They speak ill about themselves so much that they see nothing good in themselves. That's why we'll discuss this matter as it was revealed to us.

When my professors started this topic, they condemned Africans vehemently for the stupidity they have shown toward themselves. They asked me a question: Paul, is there no evil in science and technology? Is there no healing and killing medicines in white science? So, I answered: Surely there are.

This topic continued the discussion of why Africa has not developed yet. A major factor in why Africa is trailing the rest of the world is the fact that Africans were so quick to abandon everything they knew before Europeans came to them. They didn't choose between what was necessary to preserve and not to preserve; rather, they trashed everything they knew.

While hearing these things (2006-2008), I had no job nor money to come to the US where I wrote this book, but the Spirit said I would go to the Western world to see things for myself. He said I would leave my children with my wife to travel around the world, but the word of the Spirit was laughable because I couldn't imagine how this was going to happen.

Almost seven years after I received the travel prophecy, I finally came to the US in November 2013. I returned to the US in August of the following year, where I stayed until this Wednesday, July 10, 2024, as I'm writing this story tonight in Sacramento, California, USA.

One shocking thing that I found in the US is the Halloween festival. The first time I saw people dressed in scary customs, I was astonished to see that the self-proclaimed best Christian nation on earth would permit such demonic festivity while spreading the gospel to all nations, telling the people about the practices of satanism. They taught the people that their cultural ways of life were evil and satanic, but they preserved theirs.

The Americans or Westerners who introduced the Bible to Africans preached against killing fellow humans, but they fight wars every day and make weapons of mass destruction all the time. Everything they preached against is what they master doing.

After seeing all this, I realized why the Spirit of God told me to come to the West.

The Spirit revealed that Africans didn't correctly use

their willpower to unveil their sciences. Thus, their sciences remained largely dormant and have continued to be called dark science because they don't benefit the masses as white science does.

So, the Spirit took me on a tour of comparison. He said when an African uses herbs to kill someone, it is called a witch, but when a Westerner uses a drug or any chemical to kill someone, it is called poison. When an African uses a typhoon to communicate with another, it is called witch-talking [a taphoon was a new word the Spirit dictated to me to write as it is what African scientists use to communicate over long distances]. Still, when a Westerner uses the telephone to communicate with another, it is called phone talking. When an African uses any herb to heal another, it is called unscientific, but Dominic. Still, when a Westerner processes the herbs into a tablet or liquid, it is called scientific and best practice.

The Spirit demonstrated that African herbs or sciences are not all evil; instead, they are in their infant and unorganized stages. He said the Europeans were once like that, but they didn't stop changing their methods. They did so by exposing their discoveries to the public and inviting others to join in making every discovery better.

The other part of this African study led me to understand the spread of dark science among people, which is called spiritual initiations. This means that dark knowledge is widespread among the people, but it can be nurtured and grown into physical science to benefit the people of Africa and the world.

Unfortunately, explaining this is difficult in peaceful

science; instead, it is the harmful science of chemical study. Still, in the African setting, it is witchcraft, but in the Western setting, it is food poisoning.

Before this day, I had been taking lessons on how the prophets can see, but this time, I was brought to the class for healing.

I was lying down at my house. Suddenly, the Spirit raised me to my feet and thrust me to walk. I was used to it by now, so I started to go. I went to my paternal brother's house, where I met them, ready to eat. My brother called me to join him in eating, but I was stuck at his house entry. So, he knew that the Spirit was in control of me, which is why he would keep his eyes on me to see what my next action would be. I also didn't know why the Spirit of God brought me to my brother's house.

But in a moment, one of their daughters screamed to the mother and said there was pain in her stomach. While the mom was asking her for more understanding, the little girl ran past me to vomit near the house.

She was still screaming with excruciation, and her parents were contemplating taking her to the clinic. Just within that time, a power came from heaven to my mouth, and I began to tell the parents what was happening.

Firstly, I called the little girl and healed her, stretching out only my right hand to pronounce her healed. After that, I told them to ask their other daughter, who would tell them exactly what had happened, so they did.

She told them that her cousin was a witch who put some-thing in their food to conjure the little girl into their society.

The parents didn't believe what she said, so they went to

different Spiritual persons called Prophets and Prophetesses and got the same answer.

It was after this Spiritual demo that I fully understood the message to Africans. Africans were told to stop eating together from the same bowl or plate. Africans must stop taking incanted things from Spiritualists, who give these things in the name of healing and protection items meant for the people and those people's families.

Africans were advised that Spiritual centers called churches and whatever name they have should be treated as solution centers, just like hospitals.

These centers must be visited only by those experiencing critical issues without medical solutions.

These centers aid in the spread of Spiritual problems people face. The cassava, orange, biscuit, apple juice, or anything you obtain from these places is incanted with powers beyond people's eyes. When these powers enter the body through the physical materials, they react to every person's spirit differently.

In short, the Spirit of God said that the materials people receive from these centers are why Africa is infested with Spiritual churches and other spirits that act good and evil.

Also, the food people eat together helps spread other spirits that are harmful to the prosperity of many people because the saliva from some people's mouths is contaminated with their powers. The effects can be good or bad, but it's better to avoid food sharing.

Also, my professor emphasized that for those who may experience non-medical problems and go to any prophetic temple, whatever they get from there to eat or drink should not be given to friends and family members because the powers in those foods may react differently in each person's body.

I have a living story because I visited a prophetic center where many people went before me and even during my time. Strangely, what happened to me because I went there didn't happen to all the people who went there. My late wife and I went through the same rituals, but she didn't experience what happened to me that provoked God's coming down to free me and teach me about them.

Science would call this the spread of *communicable diseases*, but in Spiritual terms, it means the spread of Spiritual maggots. Spiritual maggots are harmful forces to the human body. They range from frequent nightmares to frequent illnesses, possibly spiritual ministering in dreams and real life, often referred to as witchcraft activities.

The last word of the Spirit was that even Spiritualists do not know exactly how the things they offer work in people's bodies since these are physical materials the spirits use to connect to humans to do many things in their lives.

The scenario is like what humans see in the science world. Medical scientists tell people that one specific medication can solve different problems while the same medication has side effects. Side effects refer to the possible adverse harms the medication could cause while solving a problem. Likewise, spiritually administered materials do have positive and negative effects on people.

Cultures and Traditions

This topic should have been the first of the study of our universe system, but I delayed it because I wanted to suspend people's perceptions about this ministry's work. I didn't want anyone to think that this ministry was about promoting Satanism. I wanted everyone to see the true picture of this ministry before revealing the works of the gods that got mankind to the place he is today. Still, this is not to exalt the gods but to reveal the truth about them so that mankind can see why God must destroy their works.

You must have learned by this time that Lucifer fled from Heaven with a few other men. There was no woman among them.

Why didn't women follow them?

Well, a simple analogy would help us understand this. They were not ready by then. They were the green fruits hanging in the tree that couldn't fall even when the tree was shaken. The men were the ripe fruits that could fall at the slightest touch. The men were the first angels God made before the women, so the men have grown well to make hard decisions by themselves, while the women were still young enough not to make that decision to move by themselves. So, Lucifer, later Satan, blamed the women for not joining the men.

One major reason Satan blamed the women for not joining the men was that the women refused to use the power of autonomy God put in them. It is the willingness to move or do something by yourself. The women didn't want to move out of Heaven yet, so their unwillingness made it impossible for Lucifer to force them out, not even one He was able to force out.

Do you see the role willingness plays in spiritual works? The same reason God gave us the power to choose or reject. Willingness gives the spirit free access to our body, while unwillingness poses difficulties in their way to access our body. This can be expanded on when we reach the discussion of committing sins.

So, the men came down and established their enclave closer to the physical earth. Their proximity to us gives them greater access to us. Their coming close to the earth was reported in the Bible as Satan fell to the earth. Still, He is invisible to mankind on this earth.

Let's not forget the fact that God had thrown us out of His living place already, so man was left in the hands of Satan. It was God's angry decision to let man suffer under Satan to learn a lesson before reconciliation could happen.

Well, Satan, the King of all, had to make rules to govern everyone: the angels under Him and the man who would become their tool.

So, Satan established the rules referred to as culteur (Cut along or cut along God's laws). This is the word that later became culture.

Previously, Satan had appointed one archangel called "Alasaman" to oversee the works of the four angels of His kind, who Satan appointed to oversee the four sides of the earth.

So, the laws He established were to be traded (exchanged) among the four archangels of His. This trading system was referred to as tradition or exchange or trapedition (Our trading or exchanges).

Thus, the four archangels had to appoint other angels to serve and report to them, as well as they reported to Satan. These other under-servants who oversaw the establishment of kingdoms in the physical earth had to make other under-servant appointments to oversee the clans in the kingdoms. This is how the hierarchical order of Satan's government looks to get to one single Satan's agent that oversees one individual in the world today.

These were the forces of God that made laws to govern the human world, and they established rules for violations and repercussions. Some of these laws violate the freedom of God in many situations, such as the law of dispensing knowledge called science. They're the ones who created boundaries among humans, which is why some humans receive science faster than others. Still, there is a secret thing about sex that cannot be discussed at this moment since this ministry is too young to go into disclosing this deep secret.

So, many things happening to us are the work of these gods. They're constantly punishing people in violation of the laws they set up for our ancestral fathers, but now we're not obeying them for the reason of Christianity.

When God reported the stories about Spirituality and Physicality, He juxtaposed them all. He reported Spirituality for things that happened in the Spirit world and Physicality for things that would come into the physical world.

God's style of juxtaposition made the Bible seem contradictory. For example, the Bible accounts for how Adam's and Eve's children populated the earth or how Noah's children populated the earth. Still, laws of sex boundaries emerged somewhere along the line. The question is: Who made the laws later?

Another example is God's disapproval of a man killing another man, but God sent the Israelites to war to kill other humans. The question is: Who introduced wars into the human world before God ever came to earth?

Example three is the argument about Christianity and Islamism when there are reports of God's archangel, Gabriel, in the lives of both.

Some of the activities of these gods are in other stories we have.

What are the mechanics of our body system?

Listen, my people, if I tell you that spirituality is real, please don't doubt me. I tell you this: our existence is controlled by forces we cannot see with our eyes. It is a pity for anyone to doubt what controls our universe. It is a pity for anyone to say that there is no God. It is a pity for anyone to say he/she can do anything he/she likes without the power of Heaven falling on him/her. It is a pity for anyone to say that we were created out of nowhere. It is a pity for anyone to say that this world would not end.

I suffered a lot just so the Spirit would prove that whatever we have read in the Bible is true. The Spirit said I had to suffer several pains and humiliation to get all the answers and believe that all the questions I asked about how God inspired the Bible were actual. That's why the process of making me was excruciating.

It is a pity that many people would not have the opportunity to experience the power of God in the way I did.

In this story, we'll explain how everything happens to our bodies.

Having listened to me earlier about the manifestations on me by the Spirit, you must have known already that whatever I report here has been practically demonstrated on me before now.

As I said earlier in one of my stories, the Spirit of God usually started acting on me before He would explain what He had demonstrated to me, so the following mechanics of our body system are not different.

But what is the body's mechanics? The body's mechanics in this story represent how we breathe, talk, sing, walk, lie down, wake up, sneeze, cough, get sex power, and so on.

Before going into that, let's explain something in communication science called antennae or poles. An antenna or pole is a device constructed somewhere to receive, process, and send information between stations. A station is a place with many communication devices or terminals.

I'm not a trained professional in communication science, so the definitions I gave here came exactly from the Spirit of God.

That's why the first thing done to my body was to build a station inside me, with several antennae in every part.

How did I know? Well, in December 2005, when I was carried to Pastor Solomon Adeleke's house, where he and another Pastor, Gbesee, were praying for me, I fainted. While in that sleeping condition, my eyes were physically closed on the outside but opened into the Spirit realm, where I saw the three power balls enter me. Each of them looked like a globe.

They were the satellite stations brought to earth by spiritual technicians to my body so that God could connect to His servant, who would also connect to Him. These would enable me, the servant, to hear the voices of the Spirits and the messengers, calling themselves professors or lecturers, who came through these media to speak to me.

Right after they entered me, I jumped up and began to prophesy for the first time. I confessed my visit to a prophetess, saw something of the past, and spoke about it.

These power balls represented the three vehicles for the crews of technicians who constructed a station and several antennae inside my body. These communication centers would later play a crucial role in everything that would happen to me in the following scenarios. These scenarios were scary to me from the beginning, and it took me a long time to get used to them.

From January 2006 to the middle of 2008, every day, wherever I was, whatever I wanted to do or say, I would feel a power enabling me.

For example, if I wanted to wake up from bed, I would feel a rush of air coming out of my mouth like a yawn. I would feel things moving inside every part of my body. One such energy would start from my fingers and run through my hands to my mouth before puffing out. The same would happen to my toes and run through my feet, while others run from my stomach to my mouth before puffing out. As these energies move through my body parts, I stretch, turn on every side of the bed, and release bunches of air, which we do as a yawn every morning to get out of bed.

But as these energies leave my body in the form of yawning, there comes another power I could feel while it's entering through my mouth and nose.

After these exchanges, I could feel the enabling powers that made me wake up and walk.

You know, I'm not only having difficulty explaining how the whole process works with us humans, but I'm also feeling weird about explaining it all because I seem not to believe that my listeners would understand exactly what I'm putting in a perspective here.

These exchanges begin immediately when I open my eyes or am about to open my eyes.

The angels of God explained to me that, in the Spirit world, there are spirits of brighter light, dim light, darkness, and half-darkness. So, as darkness falls slowly, that's the same way the spirits of darkness descend to earth to enter the body. Among those spirits of darkness are the ones responsible for fatigue and sleep. So, as every human gets ready to open their eyes to daylight, the spirits of sleep and others must leave the body to give way to the spirits of the locomotive (walking and talking).

Since these spirits are a bunch of different spirits, such as those for darkness, sleep, repairs, dreams, and others, they would leave together in a single ride like a company's workers do every morning and evening when they ride on a bus to arrive at the company's site together before disembarking to spread out to their various workstations or when they go back home on a bus after work to go to their various houses.

Their departure creates a force in the mouth, which we feel as a yawn. We also feel the same in our noses, as if a puff of air comes out of us when we're tired or hungry.

Speaking of hunger and tiredness brings us to other scenarios. The yawn we feel when we're hungry is the departure and incoming of spirits responsible for different things when the body needs food. There are spirits responsible for holding up life while our body is going out of food.

These spirits of hunger would continue coming and going according to their ability to withstand hunger. So, the less food in our body, the less the power to hold the body. That is, the spirit of sustaining life decreases in strength slowly as the body loses food inside it.

So, we won't stop yawning if we're hungry, which is the opening of the mouth to let in and out large bunches of spirit workers.

The same applies to the enabling spirits that make us walk, talk, sing, write, cut, even have sex, and do or say anything in this world.

The sex spirits would come down on us to arouse us [make the man's thing stand or the woman feels horny] and provide us with all the power we need to make love.

The sex spirits are in the class of death spirits. They flow into us slowly and slowly until they fill the vacuum in us to accomplish what they came to do. The sex spirits don't like to be interrupted as all others.

The first demonstration on me came when I woke up one morning, and I began to feel the flow of air power into my body, going straight to my penis and enabling it to stand up right away. Since I was accustomed to the working of the Spirit by this time, I knew it was another demo.

My penis remained standing for a little while before the air power began to flow out of me again. The flowing process slowly deflated my penis before a voice came down to educate me on how mankind gets sex power.

The second demo was about sex sin.

By this time, we were in a prayer center owned by a prophetess. While service was going on, suddenly, the flow of sex power came down on me, and I gained an erection in the church. I didn't only have an erection, but I received excruciating urges in my body. It was so intense that I called my wife [may her soul rest in peace] and told her that I needed to have sex. She was shocked and didn't want to hear it from me for the second time, saying, "Can't you see that we're in service? Where can we do that even if I should grant you your wish?"

I was so persistent and became a distraction to her, but she resisted strongly, saying it was disgusting to her, especially since we were in church.

I may have caused a nuisance, but the situation did not move the congregation because the Prophetess had told everyone earlier that I was not crazy but going through a spiritual transformation. So, once my wife was attending to me, the church continued.

Thus, right after battling with my wife, the spirit came down on me even while the church was going on, and I was told about the spirit of promiscuity.

. . .

The spirit of promiscuity is called a random sex spirit in the Spirit realm and is a real spirit that is forbidden to talk about under the laws of the gods. Since mankind is under the laws of the gods, we cannot go further with the issue of the random sex spirit.

But what is important to know is that humanity continues to face many difficulties because of these laws of the gods. Under the laws of the gods, marriage must be respected because it was formulated under the law of trade, which is one aspect of the sell-and-buy system in the world.

That's why spirit men inspired human-men parents with the idea that human men should trade (sell) their daughters out to other men who would buy to own the daughters as properties and tools for them to use as they liked.

The system of owning women was one of many punishments for human women since their spiritual representatives, spirit women, refused to join the spirit men when the men came down from Heaven to establish an enclave for themselves to rule over the world.

So, as the world grows into loving promiscuity, the practice of loving from here and there, even refusing to marry, brings about a battle between the spirits against marriage and the ones in favor of it. That's why the different misfortunes that befall us every day, no matter where we are and our race, come from the battles of the different gods and goddesses of our forefathers.

No one must fool himself that the big God is in the business of punishing people on earth. He has only one punishment for us at the end of this world system controlled by the gods doing their ways.

However, there are rare instances when the big God sends His army of intervention to arrest some situations befalling His chosen ones.

There are singing spirits in the Spirit realm. They are the spirits of music or amusement. They existed in ancient days and had their chosen ones who would continue to make music to amuse their souls.

They inspire music from all over the world. Thus, the repented inspire godly music, while the unrepented inspire secular music.

All the spirits inspire music the same. That's why when a Christian singer backslides to the secular world, he/she goes with the same musical talent. When a non-Christian singer chooses to convert to Christianity, he/she goes with the singing talent so that we can say he/she is using it for God.

Believe me, I received a demo for music making as well.

Before then, I had no idea how to make music, but when the day came, the singing spirit called Angel came down to teach me a few pieces.

In my studies, I would feel the flow of air building up inside my mouth, and my mouth would hold it like someone holding water to gaggle. To my surprise, my mouth would remain pumped up with air when the air power in my mouth starts turning my tongue and lips to make music. It did it in such a way that it was like a natural person teaching a music tutorial.

The spirit trained me slowly, while making mistakes, just the same way I have seen a church choir's musical practice.

This took place repeatedly until I mastered the first music that I can sing up to now titled, "*When I Look Up to Heaven, I see the Son of Man.*"

After I had mastered my song, the angel told me it was a music-making class, but by then, I had already known what was going on with me.

At last, He said that all spirits or angels, no matter which group they belong to, know how to make music, but the one difference is the question of which power is being amused or entertained. He said music, with many of Jesus's components, has greater power to invoke the good spirits and drive away the wicked ones because that's how the system is.

There are death spirits in the Spirit realm. They come from the Department of Illness.

In my studies, they take three primary forms: crawling smoke, tongues of fire, and rising cold.

These three forms were demonstrated to me. As usual, I didn't know what it was when I would feel a choking smoke entering my nostrils as soon as I lay my head down on the mattress that was on the floor, so I would jump out of bed immediately in fear of being choked to death in my sleep.

The invisible smoke that I could feel entering my nostrils would begin to seep down my throat, and as it reached my heart, I would feel like I was about to die. That's how it happened, but I didn't allow much of it for long because it was suffocating.

The spirit later told me that the smoke death is one kind of death spirit that crawls or drags along the ground, so it is the one that kills people while they're on the ground. It chokes people to death.

He said the fire death that I felt falling on my skin like sparks of fire was one kind of death that kills people with a striking hit. It is the fastest death kind. It is associated with accidents such as gunshots, knife stabbing, falling from a height, being hit by an object, and anything other than sleep and sickness.

The cold death comes through the feet and rises through the body. It is associated with sickness.

I felt it under my feet for the first time and thought I was getting sick with a fever. I shivered as it rose through my body, whether I was standing, sitting, or lying down. Then the voice came down to explain that it was the third kind of death for sick people.

He said there are times when both cold death and smoke death take down some people who have been sick for a long time and are lying down on the ground. Thus, smoke death is a crawling type that hits people lying on the ground, but cold death climbs altitudes, so it kills sick people lying on top of anything raised high, like a bed.

How are we born with infirmities?

Please forgive us for this storytelling we're about to do. The intention of this storytelling is not to shame our disability community. The truth is that this topic extends beyond the disability community. Rather, it includes all of us.

So, let's understand what infirmity is. Regardless of its dictionary meaning, the Spirit considered infirmity to be any unacceptable condition on anyone that renders the person incapable of doing certain things better. So, there are two sides to infirmities. They are physical and spiritual.

Physical infirmities are visible to human eyes, such as being crippled, deaf and dumb, blind, stammering, having epilepsies, and any of such things.

Spiritual infirmities are invisible conditions every human suffers. They are such things as high & low sexual urges, sensuality, alcoholism, anger, gossip, violence, high & low pitch voice, and other habits people are born with, which define them but could bring them troubles and unhappiness in any way.

So, how do these things happen to us? The answer lies in what happens in the Spiritual world even before we were born. They are the results of Spiritual inductions we, humans, undergo in the spirit realm before birth.

Unfortunately, this would take us back to biblical reports about God and His angels.

When He created the angels, He taught them everything He knew except a few things, including life.

Only God knows what life is, but the angels know how to use it.

This scenario is like the relationship between users and inventors. An inventor can teach people how to use what he/she has invented. This explains how we can use a phone or drive a car without knowing how it was made.

So, the many things God taught His children, the angels, including making humans and everything about humans, cause the bad angels to influence creations. Apart from making humans, the things to do **for** humans [help humans], **with** humans [talk, walk, work, sing with humans], and **against** humans [breakdown humans] are separate creations.

Therefore, the spirits are responsible for God's day-to-day work. They created us humans and have several departments that work on everything related to human creation.

I think it is simple to understand from our factory setup system. A factory has many departments and sections that a single product goes through from start to finish.

Well, God taught the angels for the good work He wanted to do in the world, but those who deviated from His goodness went out of His sight with the knowledge He gave them. They would later establish their separate places to use everything He taught them.

Still, we have another story that explains how God integrated the angels together so that they work autonomously and coordinatively. We said this system integration made it impossible for God to completely do away with Satan and the others.

Adding to our previous report concerning integration, God's continuous use of Satan appears in the Bible as Job's story. People called it Job, with the 'O' sound, but it means job, as in work.

The way the Bible reports that Satan is still part of Heavenly works is the story saying Satan was found among the Heavenly angels during a meeting with God, and God asked

Him, Satan, what He was doing in the earth. This represents how Satan remained an integral part of the system that runs the earth.

So, while Satan remains God's unfavorable son, He remains part of the system of creation for God. He is one of the departments or sections of the factory God set up before the so-called breakaway came. We call it a so-called breakaway because Satan is still useful to those who don't want Him since the system was integrated and is yet to be separated. The period designated for separation is called the end of our world system.

Now, here is the answer we've been waiting for.

All the imperfect ways in us are the works of Satan and His men. All the infirmities we have are from Satan and His men, with wicked women joining later.

Thus, God has no hand in creating cripples or deaf and dumps or blinds, or with sexual itches and no/low urges. These are the works of the gods of our lands. These are the different ways they manifest punishments unto us because of the laws we have broken and continue to break.

When the Spirit of God brought this lesson to me in the years 2006-2008, He said God gave Him a question to give me and for me to ask everyone: Doesn't the Bible say God made everything and it was good? He said, if that is true, then why would God make anyone that would suffer in the world or regret being born in the first place?

Reincarnation and Resemblance

There is a belief among several tribes that a dead person can come back.

Also, there is a belief about the dead being born again because a new baby resembles the dead family member.

Now is the time for us to understand how all this works.

In our story, 'How are we born with infirmities?', we revealed how God taught the angels everything concerning creation. We also revealed that the things happening in the human world are the works of the spirits of the lower kingdom. We say the spirits taught mankind everything mankind did in ancient times, which is called culture and tradition for all peoples.

The activities of these spirits have bred in the beliefs of reincarnation and resemblance in many societies.

Here are two cultural/traditional practices of the Chedepo people in River Gee County, Liberia, West Africa, as a case study.

There is the god of administration they have who passed down rules and regulations to govern their ways of life.

My grandfather told me that the name of the human mediator for the god and its people was called "Kayee Choloplay."

In ancient times, people traveled far and near to visit His shrine for consultations.

The first law prohibits people from cutting palm cabbage when the palm tree is not on a rice farm where rice is planted, and sprouted [the heads come out of the soil].

The consequence of any violation of the law was devastating to the entire Chedepo people.

The sign of breaking this law was a storm with lightning. Whenever the storm blew with lightning strikes, and people fell from heights, trees fell, killing or maiming people, it was proof of an unknown violator of the palm cabbage law.

Immediately, the elders gathered to cast lots to find the violator. Whoever was caught was fined some basic items, including palm oil, chicken, goat, and others. These items had to be paid in full to enable the elders to perform the prescribed rituals to appease the gods. A complete fulfillment of the payment, followed by the rituals, ended the heavy storm and lightning disasters.

The second scenario is that their god introduced them to a burial festival. During the burial proceeding, a dead person could dance to the rhymes of drumming and chanting. The dead could possibly point out anyone believed to have been responsible for the death. There is a lot that the dead person is said to do.

Well, in my school of the Spirits, I learned that when a person dies, he/she is gone forever. He/she has nothing in common with living. There are two significant reasons for this.

One: The human body is made of two parts; one is the soul, and the second is the flesh. The word 'flesh' encompasses everything, including bones, veins, blood, and every other thing of the human body.

The flesh remains here on earth, where it decays to become part of the soil once more.

Two: The soul is a spirit, and it is the engine God puts in a frame called the flesh.

Whenever the soul detaches from the body, it remains a living spirit.

Since the soul is a spirit, God often sends special angels to collect it from the earth. The spirits take it to storage, where all souls wait until judgment comes.

Therefore, the soul has nothing else to do with living beings. In fact, human souls don't remember anything of the earth, which is why Jesus told a story that when a husband and wife die, they will be like the angels in Heaven.

His answer embodied two things: one, angels do not marry, and two, angels are spirits.

So, how does a dead person dance during the burial process?

The shortest way to answer the question is that everything is a theatrical performance by spirits. The gods of the people manifest through some individuals to entertain and do the rest of the things people think the dead person does.

As for resemblance, the gods of manufacturing science have copies of every human created. This means that we on earth are photocopies of our original beings in Heaven. [See what the Latter-Day Saint's church reports as *where we come from*.]

So, the spirits of creation continue to reproduce every

man's original photo all the time, which results in resemblance.

Those who contributed to
this book

This book was first published in 2018 under the title *Interpreter's Third*.

Before I published it, I talked to many people, including pastors in the US, to get help with some scripture references, but no one wanted to associate with me on the project.

They wanted me to alter the book to be just like all Christian books, repeating the same understanding of the ancient people who interpreted God's messages in their own ways. They wanted me to speak of the Garden of Eden or the creation of black man in the same old fashion.

But later, God brought me a man from my home country, Liberia, **Apostle Abraham J. Kiamue**, who found interest in my books in 2024 after receiving one copy each. In his own words, he said to me via a messenger text: "We're in a world where the knowledge was hidden from us, but now God has raised a generation to bring His end-time messages and to reveal the unrevealed ones. That's why I'm happy to work with you to add scriptures in necessary areas. All the four books I read need scriptures to back them."

So, he urged his church, *Church of God Christian Ministry*, to form a collaborative working relationship with my ministry, Theocratic Ministry of the Lord Jesus Christ. In this working relationship, they were able to make themselves work daily to provide me with a few other scriptures, as you may find throughout the book.

Therefore, I sincerely thank Apostle Abraham Joe Kiamue and the officials who worked tirelessly to update this book with additional Bible verses.

Please meet these noble men and women of God.

1. Apostle Abraham Joe Kiamue

Apostle Kiamue, founder/general overseer of the Church of God Christian Ministry, born June 20, 1988, holds an AA degree in theology and several other diplomas and certificates in Biblical Studies.

2. Pastor P. Eric Mandeh

Pastor Eric, resident pastor and founding pastor of the Church of God Christian Ministry, was born on May 20, 1998, a high school graduate and obtained a ''C'' certificate in education.

3. Min. Ophelia M. Vonyeegar

Min. Ophelia, a choir director's assistant at the Church of God Christian Ministry, was born on March 18, 1990, and is a college dropout.

4. Sis. Keturah Nahn

Sis. Keturah Nahn was born on October 9, 1993, and obtained an AA degree in education and many other certificates in biblical studies. She is the children's ministry teacher at the Church of God Christian Ministry.

5. Min. Annie Payway

Min. Annie Payway, choir director and head at the Church of God Christian Ministry, was born on March 24, 2004, and is still in high school.

About the author

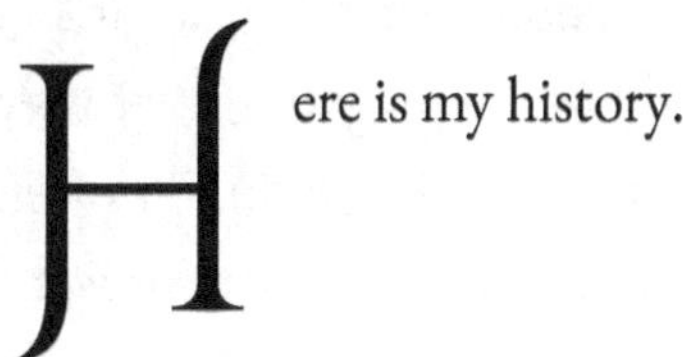

ere is my history.

Born unto Jonah Seah Tarsleh and Elizabeth T. Jah on a farm in 1970 [this is on my birth certificate by mistake but not my true birth year]; I lost my father when he was assassinated by gunshot in 1972 while I was six and reared by my grandparents in a town called "Putuken" in River Gee County, Liberia, West Africa.

I'm a Christian and a Baptist by faith since I was a teen. Still, I was baptized in the Church of Christ in 1997 after I received the first conviction that I needed to do the right thing during one of their evangelical teaching tours to me while I was in the Triechville hospital in Abidjan, Ivory Coast, with my sick son, now deceased.

Why did it take me so long to get baptized so late? Well, that is because when I first started attending church with my grandpa, who was a Baptist and with whom I had an amicable relationship more than my grandma, who was a Pentecostal member, I had so many questions in my mind about being a Christian since all the people were still doing the things they preached against every day [adultery, fornication, promiscuity, polygamy, drunkenness, lying, gossiping, consulting with the devil and all the likes], including pastors who went in bed with church members. At most times, when I hear my friends jumping here and there for the joy of going to choir practices or going to church conferences, I would ask them whether they were doing that for the girls in the choir department or those in the congregation that they were having time with and talked about all the time. I often asked: Is it the primary purpose of being a Christian, or is it a secret part of serving God?

This same purpose of questioning Christian life [seeing them doing the things that they preach against] has made me cancel my first baptism, which should have been done as early as 1985 in the Providence Baptist Church, the first and biggest Baptist Church in Monrovia, Liberia, West Africa, after attending two weeks of baptismal classes in January of that year.

Even after baptizing in the Church of Christ in Triechville, Abidjan, Ivory Coast, West Africa, I still discovered sex scandals among them contrary to what they preached and separated women from men in housing. [Hopefully, I'm not mistaken about this part.] I think they sit in separate aisles in their church house during service. So, instead of remaining in their Church as I previously thought, I went back to my Effort Baptist Church in Tabou, Ivory Coast, where I served as a financial Secretary in 2004 under the caretaking administration of Bro. Robert Teally after Pastor Freeman, who had taken over from Pastor Shelton Seidee earlier, had left for Abidjan for the UN's Resettlement program.

After returning to Liberia in 2006, I served as Bookkeeper in 2008 [but the only one holding the key to the cash box based on the high level of trust] for the Messiah Mission Church School in Monrovia, Liberia.

While serving as a bookkeeper, I also taught English subjects from grades seven to nine. I also served as a member of the Church's Men's Department and was honored as Father of the Year in 2008, for which I received a certificate.

As to how much knowledge [knowledge through classroom education] I have, I'll say very little. I'm a high school graduate who served as valedictorian for my 1989 graduate class and thus obtained a government scholarship to go to the university the following year, 2000, where I wanted to do Mass Communication and Political Science, but Civil war broke out in that country, and it took my opportunity away. This was exacerbated by other factors beyond my control while living as a refugee with two kids, including the one born with disabilities. Therefore, my highest level of education is an 18-month vocational study in Bookkeeping along with computer literacy (basics of Ms-Word and Ms-Excel), basics of filing systems, and basics of small business management.

Once again, misfortune came in [misfortune—is the way

I put it all in the human setting] when I set out to acquire more knowledge of the Bible in January 2006. I registered for a two-year evangelical study at the "Maranatha Evangelical School" organized by the Tabou-Liberian Assembly of God Church, but something mysteriously happened to me on the night I returned from my first class.

On that night, I was lifted from my bed while I was asleep. At first, I was deeply asleep when I noticed myself being snatched out of my bed, just as in a dream when you seem to be flying up like a rocket. Still, when I opened my eyes in fear, I saw two hands slipping off my two hands, and to my surprise, I was actually hanging in the low ceiling of the apartment room that I rented for 40,000 CFA. I came down to the ground just when my fiancée jumped up in wails and grabbed my waist. Oops, this is the day I was changed from what I was before this incident to what I am now as a new person who hears and speaks with God.

Naturally, as you may think, I had no delights in voodoos [consultations with the magic powers] at all in all of its forms, so how I got here with the power of the Spirit is one thing of mystery.

Hmmm, this whole lifting thing that occurred to me didn't happen for anything but for a perfect reason. According to the Spirit of Christ, God allowed the lifting by the wicked forces [evil spirits] in the world to give me a practical understanding of how spirituality works, similar to how Jesus was lifted from the grave. It was also meant to provide me with a practical knowledge of how the rapture and the resurrection shall be when the end comes.

The instant change of my body was meant to help me

understand and teach how the righteous shall instantly become new people, having new bodies, and in their case, they shall not know the old things again.

Even from that day, I became pregnant with the spirit to demonstrate how Jesus' mother, Mary, was conceived with the spirit. [This is something strange living inside me from that event].

A few months after receiving the Spirit of Christ, I was made to understand that I had experienced something called a "Power encounter" on that night where the evil forces came for me to prevent me from going to study the word of God since this would make me more resilient against the evil practices in the world. Still, then the Spirit of Christ [Angel Marcus] came down from Heaven right away and rescued me from those hands that were taking me to an unknown destination where I was going to stay as a missing person for some number of weeks. I was told that if I had gone missing and come out from there, I would have been a different person who possessed magical powers to perform in the name of the Lord Jesus Christ.

So, when the angel of Christ rescued me, he said the incident didn't only expose my soul to the Kingdom of darkness; instead, it helped to impact my mind in a way that qualifies me to speak the things that I know about the dark world and the things that the Light world would pass on to me in the years to come.

So, for two and half years (2006-mid2008), I kept under the voices of the people of light (the spirits of God that delight in good things). The result has been four significant books inspired by the good Spirits, each dealing with one particular topic based on the Holy Bible while touching on all life activities today as they relate to the Bible and the world around us.

During the two-and-a-half-year period mentioned above, I was labeled by my people as insane or mentally deranged since I was doing and saying things out of the normal. But they were right because I took on the body of a man who communes with the unseen forces. In this state, I could see invisible things that anyone sitting by me couldn't see. I could hear what anyone sitting by me couldn't hear.

Even in this same state, I bought a hardback notebook to take notes and draw things, like the diagrams depicting God in His trinity. [I still have that notebook].

While I was doing all this, I kept telling them that I was taking notes from the spirits that were telling me that I was going to write these things in books unto the world and that I was going to leave Africa to go to the Western World where I would be able to explain all of what I was taking notes on.

All of these made no sense to my people, especially when I said I would go to America, which was the worst utterance out of human imagination since I didn't have a job, and even if I had one, how much would have been my salary at that time in Liberia that could give me the amount it costs to pay for a plane ticket. Yet I told them that the books would grant me a US visa but that I didn't know how to get the money to travel. Still, one sure thing was that the spirits kept telling me the time was yet to come for me to get the money, so I needed not to worry about that.

Surely, in the middle of 2008, I received a message from the spirit world that I had now graduated from the theocratic school of the Spirit and was free to go into the world to do what everyone does by finding work to do. So, I set out and got hired by a friend to teach in his computer school. Then, after three months, I got a call from the Overseer, Rev. David Gballah, of the Messiah Mission Institute, to come to audit his school's financial books since he was not getting a clear picture of what was happening there.

With my 18-month bookkeeping skills, I conducted the audit and was paid $3,000.00 Liberia Dollars @ a rate of 60:1, about $50.00 US dollars. Based on my recommendations, he found no one qualified to implement those recommendations, so he chose to hire me as a bookkeeper next to the school's female accountant.

He intended to make me the accountant [of course, I could have been just a bookkeeper]. Still, the school was like a tribal-based institution, so the administrative board didn't want to kick the lady out but accepted that I was going to have the responsibility of safekeeping the money in a secured metal box, where it must be kept until it reached 50,000.00 Liberian dollars, approximately $833.00 US dollars, as recommended by me to take to the bank while maintaining a 5,000.00 Liberian dollars for petty cash for daily activities.

I became too strict and caused others too much embarrassment, so something happened, and I had to resign after a few months.

After that, I took another Bookkeeping job in 2009 at the Cuttington University Credit Union in Gbarnga, Bong County, Central Liberia. In December 2010, I took employment at a multimillion Iron Ore mining company, Arcelor-Mittal-Liberia, as a Procurement Officer (Buyer), where I worked until August 2014, when I left to visit the US on my leave break but didn't return to Liberia due to the Ebola outbreak in that year.

How I made enough money to publish my first two books with AuthorHouse, UK, in 2013 and 2014 and to travel to the US is one case scenario meant to explain "Imposed sin," which is out of discussion now for others' privacy.

And precisely as the Spirit had earlier predicted through me, that's how I came to the United States for the first time in November 2013. It means I obtained my US visa in 2013 at the invitation of AuthorHouse, UK, to participate in a Book Signing event for my two books in Miami, Florida, USA, that year.

The job that brought me money, the receiving of a US visa without any delay, and the traveling to the US all served as the first fulfillment of the things conferred on me and predicted through me by the spirits. These predictions have been my initial strengths and are why I have a genuine mission to fulfill. That mission has just begun, for the world has a lot to hear yet, but to be made possible by those who read this book and all of my books whose purchases and other supports shall make the mission more fulfilling.

As you're set to read this book, I want you to know that I'm doing the unconventional thing (revealing materials far beyond what is available in the Bible) because I'm just a storyteller, not a biblical writer whose duty is to fill the book with scriptures.

However, based on many recommendations, I had the privilege of using the expertise of the Church of God Christian Ministry in Liberia, West Africa, to provide more scripture references in this revised version.